HAMPSHIRE

A Sense of Place

HAMPSHIRE

A Sense of Place

By Peter F. Mason • Photographs by Judy Harrison

HAMPSHIRE BOOKS

First published in 1994 by Hampshire Books

Design & typography:
Neil Crawford, Bromley Arts /Art World

HAMPSHIRE BOOKS
Official Publishers to

in association with Southgate Publishers Ltd

Southgate Publishers Ltd
Glebe House, Church Street, Crediton
Devon, EX17 2AF
Tel: 0363 777575 Fax: 0363 776007

SALES
Direct sales enquiries to Hampshire Books
at the address above

ISBN 1-85741-042-4

The author of this book is County Arts Officer for Hampshire County Council; he is writing here in a personal capacity and the views expressed are not necessarily those of the County Council.

British Library Cataloguing-in-publication Data: A CIP Catalogue Record for this book is available from the British Library.

Printed and bound in Great Britain by BPC Wheatons Ltd, Exeter, Devon.

Front cover: Butser Hill (top left); Denny Wood (top right); Hurdle making near Little Somborne (bottom left); Rose Garden, Mottisfont Abbey (bottom right).

Back cover: Fishing hut on the River Test, near Longstock.

Frontispiece: Hillier Arboretum.

ACKNOWLEDGEMENTS

I WOULD LIKE TO THANK the following for the advice and assistance they have given me during the writing of this book: The English Folk Dance and Song Society; the staff of the Local Studies Library, Hampshire County Council, Winchester; Merrick Denton-Thompson, John Holder and Mike Hughes of Hampshire County Council Planning Department; Stephen Locke, Alison Carter, and Ian Edelman of Hampshire County Council Museums; Rosemary Dunhill and Sarah Lewin of Hampshire Record Office; Elizabeth Goodall and Margot Heller of Southampton Art Gallery; Roger Watson of Traditional Arts Projects; Peter and Lynda Boulton, Peter Cuff, Freddie Emery-Wallis, Mike Hancock, Cecilia and Murray Marshall.

We also thank the following for permission to take photographs, and for permission to reproduce pictures:
Art Institute of Chicago; Lord Carnarvon; Charles Orr-Ewing; English Heritage; The Leger Galleries Ltd, London; the Martyn Gregory Gallery; The National Trust; Methuen Ltd (for permission to reproduce a cartoon from *A Leg at Each Corner* by Norman Thelwell); Southampton City Art Gallery; Tate Gallery, London; Test Valley Borough Council; Nick Redman, Archivist, Whitbread plc; and Winchester Cathedral.

Acknowledgements are due to:
the Estate of Flora Thompson; John Murray Publishers for permission to include an extract from 'Youth and Age on Beaulieu River, Hampshire' by John Betjeman; Penguin Books Ltd for permission to include an extract from *As I Walked Out One Midsummer Morning* by Laurie Lee; Richard Adams and Penguin Books Ltd for permission to include an extract from *Watership Down.*

I am also indebted to Simon Goodenough, Paul Turner and Stephen Adam and the other members of the editorial board of Hampshire Books. Finally I would like to thank the staff of the County Arts Office and my family for their support, encouragement, and tolerance during the writing of this book.

PETER F. MASON

"As you get to know Europe slowly, tasting the wines, cheeses and characters of the different countries you begin to realize that the important determinant of any culture is after all – the spirit of place.

Just as one particular vineyard will always give you a special wine with discernible characteristics so a Spain, an Italy, a Greece will always give you the same type of culture – will express itself through the human being just as it does through its wild flowers."

LAWRENCE DURRELL,
Landscape and Character

"Hampshire affords plenty of Corn, Cattle, Wool, Wood, and Iron, but is particularly esteem'd for its excellent Honey and Bacon Jts. Manufactures are Kersies and Stuffs; The air is temperate, and the Soil fertile in all sorts of Grain. As its coasts furnish Oysters, Lobsters, and other Salt-water Fish, so its Rivers abound in fresh Fish, especially Trouts. Here are many convenient Harbours, which bring a great Foreign Trade to it. And indeed, there is not a more inviting County in Great Britain, as well for Profit as Pleasure."

T. KITCHEN, c 1750

CONTENTS

St Catherine's Hill, from the Water Meadows, Winchester

CHAPTER 1

INTRODUCTION

If you were to be parachuted into any part of England, without map or compass, how would you know where you were? Of course, if you were to land near a village, town or city, you could look for a place-name but assume for the moment you landed away from a settlement or that the place-names had been erased for some reason. What clues would you look for? Landscape, in the first instance: is the area mountainous or flat, are there lakes or woods; what is the soil, and is there evidence of underlying rock forms? After that you might look at field patterns and crops: does arable or pasture predominate? What are the crops, the breeds of cattle? Do these give any clues as to where you are? Then you might look at the buildings: what is the style of the ordinary houses, farms and farm buildings; what are they made from? Are they brick, stone, or some other material; are they roofed with tiles, slate, or thatch?

These, and many other factors, are the clues by which we know our landscape – factors that differ quite dramatically across even such a small country as Britain. This book is about one part of England, and in it I attempt to show, through the landscape, architecture, and culture of Hampshire, that each and every part of the country differs, sometimes dramatically, sometimes subtly, but always in a way that helps define our everyday surroundings. It is not a guide book, nor a history of Hampshire. I have included only those things which I think help to define the county.

Some of these features have disappeared over the last fifty years and many are being removed every day of the week. It is important that we recognize them and know their value if our countryside is not to become a vast homogeneous Euro-agri-leisure park, with few discernible differences between north and south, west and east, the margins of the cities and what 'wilderness' is left. As Hampshire-born John Arlott said in his autobiography *Basingstoke Boy*[1]: "It's all too easy not to appreciate Britain in all its variety."

The English shires are integral to the cultural history of the country:

> "A most important thing, an absolutely crucial thing about the shires is that they both represented and created a sense of community. The shires became like little countries, with a social life and patriotic emotions of their own."[2]

Hampshire is the county at the heart of central southern England, the present day borders of which stretch from Havant in the east to include the New Forest in the west; from the cities of Portsmouth and Southampton in the south to Aldershot in the north. One of the largest counties in England, covering 378,000 hectares, its borders reach to within twenty miles of London, and its population numbers over one and a half million. A county which benefited from the boom years of the 1970s and 1980s, Hampshire is, by any definition, a well

Denny Wood, The New Forest

developed part of Britain. It has never been noted, as many of the peripheral regions of Britain are, for the individuality of its culture. Here there is no culinary dish as well known as Cornish pasties, or Devonshire clotted cream; no indigenous musical instrument such as the Northumbrian pipes; no nationally recognized distinctive industrial landscape to compare with Cornish tin mines or the dry stone walling of the Yorkshire Dales. Yet Hampshire does have its individual characteristics which enable it to be distinguished from the neighbouring counties of Sussex, Berkshire, Wiltshire and Dorset.

Edward Thomas, who spent many years living in Hampshire, thought it would be difficult to distinguish between the counties in Southern England. In his book *The South Country*[3] he said it would take a more intellectual eye than his to "distinguish county from county by its physical character, its architecture, its unique combination of elements". Yet

Near Binsted, watercolour by W.H. Allen (Hampshire County Museums)

From A Leg at Each Corner
by Norman Thelwell

Thomas did have a natural eye for those things which distinguish an area and which, along with the economy, folklore, history, art, literature, food and drink, make up our culture.

Culture is one of those words which can mean anything or everything. Writing in 1948, T. S. Eliot[4] asked the reader to

"... remind himself... how much is... embraced by the term culture. It includes all the characteristic activities and interests of a people: Derby Day, Henley Regatta, Cowes, the twelfth of August, a cup final, the dog races, the pin table, the dart board, Wensleydale Cheese, boiled cabbage cut into sections, beetroot in vinegar, nineteenth-century Gothic churches and the music of Elgar. The reader can make his own list."

These, for the most part, are not the things by which we define our culture today but the point of his definition remains the same. In its broadest meaning, culture is how people make sense of their values, their habits, their rituals and their creations – in fact all

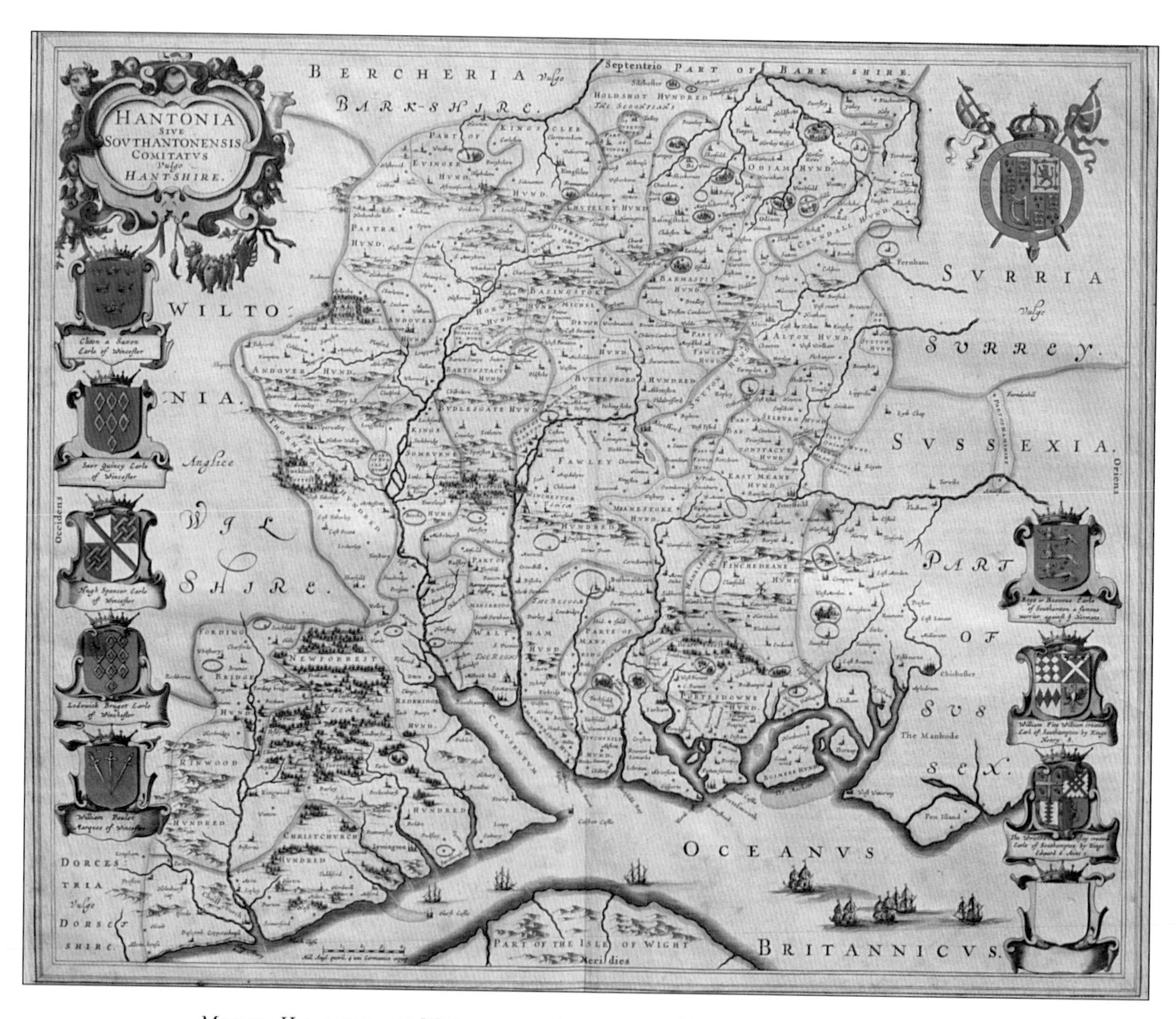

Map of Hampshire by W. Janszoon Blaeu, 1645 (Hampshire County Museums)

those things which give context to and define our lives. Culture is not something which can be frozen and displayed in a heritage museum; it is constantly changing and, in order to preserve the character of its past, we have to be conscious of its present worth and its future value.

The culture of a region is like a personality or a gene – the gene being the basic unit of heredity, evolution, and those things that distinguish each species. Some factors in a region may be unique but many are shared with one or more other regions. The individuality, or 'personality', of each region is brought about by the coming together of these characteristics in a unique combination. At the borders there may be a merging from one 'personality' to another; only where there is a clearly defined barrier, such as the sea, is there a distinctly drawn line. The 'personality' may also change within a region to some degree but where there is more in common within the region than there is with a neighbouring region then the distinctiveness of that region can still be recognized. I hope to show in this book that even where the 'personality' of a region is less obviously distinguishable from its neighbours, the distinctiveness is still present and recognizable by the coming together of individual characteristics.

For the purposes of this book I have used the boundaries of Hampshire that have existed since 1974. In other words I have not included Bournemouth and Christchurch – or the Isle of Wight. However, it is the culture of the historic Hampshire that I am writing about. Despite a few changes over the centuries, the present day boundaries of Hampshire can be seen in the Saxon arrangements for local administration of the area. The earliest reference to Hampshire in the Anglo-Saxon Chronicle is in the year 757, making "Hampshire as a unit of government and authority ... older than England, far older than any European state."[5] The Domesday survey of Hampshire in 1086 describes the shire in terms of villages and hundreds (groups of villages), which were by and large pre-conquest in origin. Geographically the county is also well defined by the catchment areas of its rivers. With the exception of the Wiltshire section of the Avon, Hampshire contains all the rivers, and their catchment areas, which flow from the mainland into the Solent, and it is only in the north and north-east of the county that rivers such as the Wey, Blackwater, Whitewater and Loddon flow towards the Thames. Hampshire is more than administrative convenience. It is a clearly definable historical and geographical entity.

Driving across Hampshire and into Wiltshire, for example, you can tell, within a few miles, where the border is. Although the chalk downs extend through the two counties, the trees and shelter belts which are common in Hampshire are scarcer in the Wiltshire landscape; rivers are fewer;

there are more dry valleys; the landscape is bleaker and apparently poorer. Hampshire's landscape appears to be richer and more luxurious.

Geology, climate, vegetation and wildlife are the main natural influences on the character of the landscape but landscape is not static and the most significant force for change has been human influence. These elements also help to determine the look and position of settlements. Along with communications and the proximity of the area to markets, the same factors help to shape the economy of a region. The relationship of it to other parts of the country and to other countries can be very significant, and so Hampshire's strategic position has been important throughout history. Winchester has been the capital of England. Southampton was a major gateway to Britain in the age of the great liners. Portsmouth, only seventy-five miles from London and a hundred miles from France, has, throughout history, played a major part in the defence of the Realm.

The reorganization of the militia in the mid eighteenth century resulted in 'The Men of Hampshire' being called to arms under the banner of the North and South Hampshire Militias, combined into the Hampshire Militia in 1853. Similarly, two eighteenth-century infantry regiments, the 37th and 67th, were by the 1780s known as the North Hampshire's and South Hampshire's, and in 1881 were joined to form the Hampshire Regiment. Hampshire's geographic position has meant that there has always been a strong military and naval presence in the county which has left its mark on the use of the land in many parts of the county.

The wealth of Hampshire, and the county's central role in affairs of state, created the conditions for more expensive materials used in the building of such masterpieces as Winchester Cathedral to be imported, and for highly skilled craftsmen to be used in their construction. Winchester Cathedral's royal patronage enabled it to attract monks whose superb artistry created some of England's finest works, such as the Winchester Bible. In later years wealthy landowners acted as patrons to writers and artists such as Shakespeare and Turner.

The landscape of Hampshire has provided inspiration to artists, writers and composers. Artists have recorded their surroundings and significant events that have taken place there, composers have tried to capture its quintessential essence, song writers have celebrated historical events, and authors have written about or set their stories in it. At no time do I claim that the accident of birth makes someone a Hampshire artist. As John Everett Millais, who was born in Southampton but considered himself a Jersey man, said, "being born in a stable would not make me a horse!"

These are the subjects of this book – the landscape and buildings of Hampshire, its art and architecture, its writers and painters, its people, their customs, food, songs and sports. Since starting to write it, I have come across numerous examples of the individuality of the area. There are so many that I have had to omit whole subjects, such as the industry and economy. Shipbuilding, for example, is probably linked with Hampshire in the minds of all, but at various times in history other industries have flourished in Hampshire for particular reasons – for instance, in the nineteenth century, Portsmouth was one of the largest corset manufacturing areas in the country. The origins of this? With husbands at sea, women provided a cheap and ready labour force, first for the making of naval uniforms and shirts, and then, with whalebone brought in through the port, the making of corsets. Another example is Burberry's, the exclusive rainwear manufacturer, which began with a

continued on page 21

Cottage at Longstock

Above Bar Street, Southampton

Weston Shore, Southampton

continued from page 17

store in Basingstoke supplying outdoor clothing for field sports. The mill in Laverstoke is an example of the continuity of family industry in Hampshire. Established by Henri Portal, a French refugee, in 1712, the Portal family still produces watermarked paper for the Bank of England at the Mill.

Michael Vlahos, Director of the Centre for the Study of Foreign Affairs at the U.S. State Department said:

"The world is customarily seen as a set of geographical regions and nation-states. This framework, however, ignores culture as the actual source of human reality. Patterns of thought and behaviour are shaped by culture; they are not the product of mere nationalism."

At a time when, on the one hand, the map of Europe is being redrawn almost daily, when in parts of the United Kingdom there is talk of independence, and when we hear much about the 'Europe of the Regions'; and, on the other hand, when McDonald's and Marks and

Basingstoke

Spencers, to name but two, build to a universal design, and identical goods can be found in High Streets right across the world; when seventy-two million people watch the same pop concert, and local cultures are submerged in a metropolitan uniformity, it is all the more important that we look afresh at that part of the world in which we ourselves live in order that we may celebrate our own culture and value its place in a common European and, indeed, world heritage. Commercial and political pressure for conformity can be more easily resisted if we recognize our strengths and take steps to build enlightened and living regional cultures.

To avoid parochialism a regional culture cannot ignore national and international trends. It will draw inspiration from a variety of places including external sources as well as its own locality and history. Products of a regional culture will often take to the international stage. It could be said that Tanita Tikaram, brought up in Basingstoke, largely a post-war town, is part of Basingstoke's culture. In 1992 the group, The Trogs, acknowledged their roots in the title of their disc, *Athens to Andover*. These modern examples from popular culture, together with the Winchester Bible, the poems of Edward Thomas, the paintings of William Shayer, Winchester Cathedral and Portchester Castle, the songs of Charles Dibdin and the music of Gerald Finzi, watercress soup, trout, and Brown Bread and Honey Ice Cream, St Catherine's Hill and the waters of the Solent, are all part of the culture of Hampshire. All these and more within this book, as well as those that I have not had space to include (and those that will be brought to my notice after it is published!), are the things that define Hampshire. They are all known to the people of Hampshire, although many of them may be taken for granted by them. They are the things that give us a sense of place and individuality in an ever more uniform world. It is also by these things that our visitor parachuted into the county will know the area.

Near Hursley

CHAPTER 2

THE LAND

DRIVING INTO HAMPSHIRE on the A34, a few miles south of Newbury, woodland is left behind and the countryside opens out to reveal the open slopes of Beacon Hill on the right, and the steep escarpment of Watership Down on the left. Chalk downland like this, and the large fields leading up to it, is typical of much of Hampshire. This band stretches south and eastwards in a broad swathe that eventually runs out of the county along the ridge of Portsdown Hill to the north of Portsmouth.

In contrast, if you drive across the border from Dorset, a very different landscape is seen. Here the roads cross uncultivated heathland covered with heather, gorse and bracken, and pass through the magnificent woodland which is so characteristic of the New Forest.

The most spectacular way to arrive in Hampshire is from the sea. Even today, when car ferries carry passengers by the thousand across the Channel to and from France, the approach past the Needles and Hurst Spit or around the eastern end of the Isle of Wight and into the sheltered waters of the Solent is one of the most dramatic landfalls in Britain.

From the downland, heaths, and forests already mentioned, to the numerous river valleys that penetrate deep into the county from the South, Hampshire's is a varied landscape and part of Hampshire's uniqueness is due precisely to this great range of countryside. Geology and climate are the main natural influences on the character of the landscape. Chalk underlies half the county, creating the downland which is probably the most distinctive feature of Hampshire's landscape – in particular the North Hampshire Downs, the river valleys of the Meon, Itchen and Test, and the South Downs which extend from Sussex into Hampshire as far as Winchester. Gravels, sands and clays lie along the coast, and these reach their greatest extent under the New Forest. Another similar but smaller area can be seen in the heathlands of Yateley Common, and Bramshill and Woolmer Forests in the north-east of the county.

The other great feature of Hampshire is the coastline which stretches for seventy miles from Barton on Sea in the west to Sandy Point on Hayling Island in the east. Here there are no dramatic cliffs and Hampshire's coastline has been witness to a constant round of erosion and deposition of sand and shingle. Originally a river valley in the land mass that until 7000 BC joined Hampshire and the Isle of Wight, the Solent provides extensive and deep natural harbours and inlets which, with four tides a day, provide the best harbours on the south coast of England.

After the geology and climate it is human influence that has been the most significant force for change on the landscape. This process has been going on since Mesolithic and

Neolithic farmers first began to clear the land more than seven thousand years ago. At this time Hampshire's landscape was covered by forests of oak, elm, lime, ash, birch, hazel and alder. In the Neolithic period (4000 BC to 1800 BC) hunting and gathering gave way slowly to more settled arable and pastoral farming. The chalk downlands, being easier to work, were cleared of forests first, and so the process of producing the landscape we know today began.

An extensive period, from the end of the Bronze Age in 800 BC to the end of the Iron Age in the first century BC, saw the building and occupation of the hill forts which are such a feature of the Hampshire landscape today. Thirty hill forts can still be seen, often topped with clumps of trees, probably the best known being those at Old Winchester Hill, Danebury, St Catherine's Hill and Beacon Hill.

The heathlands of north-east Hampshire and parts of the New Forest may have been created by

clearance and exhaustion of the light soils in the Bronze Age. These areas were colonized when the exposed chalk lands suffered top soil erosion. Among other events in the Bronze and Iron Ages significant for today's Hampshire landscape was the introduction of cereal farming on a relatively large scale. Aerial photographs show that there was as much land under cultivation on the chalk lands in the late Iron Age and the Roman period as there is today.

The Romans must have found in Hampshire a cleared landscape – a landscape of ploughed land and pasture on, and adjacent to, the downs – and it appears that they did little to modify it. After the Roman invasion the rural economy remained much the same as it was in the Iron Age in many areas, although large villas were established in the valleys and on the fringes of the downland. The Romans introduced sweet chestnut plantations which they coppiced in order to supply timber to fire the kilns used in

Heathland, The New Forest

From the 'Zig-Zag', Selbourne

making pottery, tiles and bricks, and for heating their bath houses. Roads were the most lasting mark on the landscape left by the Romans and we will look at these later in this chapter.

The Romans developed a series of forts along the south coast, of which Portchester Castle is the finest, to protect England from attack by the Saxons but in the early fifth century the Roman administration finally crumbled when the army was withdrawn. After the Saxon migrations, the new settlers lived on the downs and along the river valleys, and that great feature of the English rural scene, the village, began to evolve. By the eleventh century many of the villages on the map of England today existed and their names can be seen in the Domesday Book of 1086.

More woodland was cleared and a new generation of ploughs brought the heavier and more fertile soils of the river valleys into cultivation. Between the fifth and eleventh centuries the woodland in Hampshire

Deer at Bolderwood, The New Forest

was reduced by some fifty percent. Little direct evidence of the agriculture of this period remains in the landscape today, because the Saxons may have farmed Roman and prehistoric fields, and because Saxon fields have been overlayed with the farming of succeeding centuries.

The Norman Conquest of 1066, which resulted in such dramatic changes in political and social life, affected the landscape far less. In the countryside the elements of continuity stand out, villagers farming the land as they had done in the preceding centuries.

The most significant and lasting change to the landscape in Hampshire was the designation of a large area of south-west Hampshire as a hunting forest. Called the New Forest when William I appropriated the land in the eleventh century, it was one of a number of such royal parks in Hampshire where the fauna, in particular the deer, became the preserve of royal hunting parties.

Although large areas of land had begun to come under the ownership of one lord in the late Saxon period, this trend accelerated, and became very significant, under the Normans. The amount of land owned by the church was to be of particular importance to the Hampshire landscape:

"The estates of lay owners might vary with political change. Manors owned by ecclesiastics were not usually subject to such political hazards and in Hampshire a fundamental and unchanging feature of the economy of the county, even as recently as the mid nineteenth century, was the large proportion of land, the many manors owned by the Church."[1]

During the twelfth and thirteenth centuries it was the swelling agricultural surpluses which financed the building or re-building of the great castles, cathedrals, monasteries and churches, which are the main legacy of the Normans.

Population growth in the countryside greatly increased the demand for land. Villages expanded, fresh areas of arable land were carved out of common land, woods and heaths, and it was in this period that the open field system of agriculture reached its peak in Hampshire. By the thirteenth and fourteenth centuries open fields were being divided up into smaller fields and enclosed with hedges, banks and ditches. In addition the creation of extensive sheep walks on the downs led to the complete clearance of some villages. Old Burghclere, in the north of the county, was one such place.

A system of watering riverside meadows was developed in the mid sixteenth century in order to produce an early crop of grass in late March to help the increased number of sheep to survive the lack of late winter and early spring fodder. Water meadows, un-watered today, survive as common land at Stockbridge, where, a mile away, adjacent to Woolbury Ring, there is corresponding downland. The grazing rights for both these

continued on page 34

SHEEP ON BEACON HILL

MOTTISFONT ABBEY GARDEN

continued from page 31

commons are still allocated by the medieval Courts Leet and Baron.

There has been a constant ebb and flow over the centuries in the balance between arable and pasture in Hampshire. Sheep farming reached peaks in the early thirteenth century and again in the fourteenth and fifteenth centuries. On the other hand Daniel Defoe noted in 1724 that a great deal of downland had been converted from sheep walks to wheatland. By the 1870s and 1880s pasture was again dominant and the sheep management of the downs in Hampshire and the south had a reputation that was unsurpassed.

In addition to the New Forest, there were at one time a number of great forests in Hampshire, such as the Forest of Bere, Alice Holt Forest, and Woolmer Forest. Woodland clearance has taken place at various times in history but never more so than in the seventeenth and eighteenth centuries when a great deal of timber was felled in order to supply Hampshire's

shipbuilding industry. For example, in 1784, one thousand loads were taken from Alice Holt Forest. The depletion reached such an extent that new planting took place in the Forest of Bere and elsewhere, thus creating the woodlands of today.

Modern farming had its origins in the changes in farming practice in the eighteenth and early nineteenth centuries. In the early eighteenth century the introduction of clover, sainfoin and turnips helped to increase productivity, and the mid eighteenth century saw the introduction of new machinery such as Jethro Tull's seed drill. The second half of the eighteenth century saw a revolution that was as profound in the rural areas of England as the Industrial Revolution when mechanization was widely introduced and enclosures were completed. No other period of history has had such a significant effect on the rural population, and the effects were as keenly felt in Hampshire as anywhere.

The last hundred years have seen the continuing development of mechanization and the consequent enlargement of fields. More sophisticated farming techniques have enabled large areas of downland to be ploughed, and it is only with recent grain surpluses that some of this is being returned to pasture.

There is no aspect of the landscape of Hampshire today which better reflects the shifting pattern of human activity than the network of lanes, tracks and paths which criss-cross the county. Once major routes may now be insignificant tracks and former sheep droves may be main roads. In prehistoric times tracks connected hill forts and avoided the heavily wooded and marshy valleys, keeping to the higher ground and creating the oldest existing roads – the ridgeways. One of these, the Harrow Way, ran from the Kent coast across the face of Southern England. The track entered the county near Farnham, passed south of Basingstoke, through Andover, and left the county near Quarley. Much of its route is metalled today.

The Romans laid out an extensive road system, built initially for the rapid movement of the occupying Roman armies. At the hub of this in Hampshire were the towns of Winchester and Silchester. Roads also linked a number of small market towns. Neatham, near Alton, was a small defended settlement of this type and there may have been others at Havant, Wickham and East Anton, near Andover. In a few cases the road causeway and its flanking ditches survive, visible as earthworks, and many modern roads follow, for at least part of their route, the same road as their Roman predecessors – among these are the A33, A30, and B3420.

After the collapse of the Roman occupation these roads fell into disuse. The native population and the Saxon immigrants preferred to use new tracks and paths linking villages, hamlets and farms. These routes still account for the majority of footpaths,

bridle tracks and minor roads in use today, although some diversions were made in subsequent centuries as fields were rationalized – in particular when open fields were enclosed.

A number of fairs held in Hampshire were of national importance from the fifteenth to at least the eighteenth century, in particular that held at Weyhill, near Andover. A new network of routes developed to serve them, at times coinciding with earlier tracks. In all, no less than eight roads converged on Weyhill, bringing traffic from Farnham and the east, Winchester, Southampton, Salisbury, Amesbury and from the west, Marlborough, Hungerford and Newbury. These 'drift roads' were wide in order to accommodate the flocks of sheep and other animals, and generally avoided settlements en route.

A major development in travel came with the coaching routes of the seventeenth and eighteenth centuries. Destinations changed and the focus

The Portsmouth Fly *by Thomas Rowlandson*
(Leger Galleries Ltd)

for the new and improved routes became London. Some of these routes are still important today, especially the London to Exeter road, and the routes to Portsmouth, Winchester and Southampton. By the beginning of the nineteenth century there were over twenty new turnpike roads in the county. Evidence of their existence can be seen in surviving milestones and toll-houses, often found on roads which have been by-passed by later routes.

The coming of canals had a less significant and lasting effect on the landscape of Hampshire. River transport was important in the early days of the history of the county, and the River Itchen was made navigable to Alresford in the early thirteenth century. It fell into decay and it was not until 1710 that the river was further improved to enable barges to reach Winchester. The River Avon was improved between 1665 and 1684 to enable shipping to reach Salisbury from Christchurch, but it was never fully utilized and its maintenance was stopped in 1772.

The Basingstoke Canal, used today by pleasure craft and restored up to the Greywell Tunnel, was built early in the nineteenth century to connect what was then a small market town with London Docks, seventy-one miles and three or four days journey away. A canal also ran from where the River Test joins the Solent to Andover. Opened in 1794, the Andover Canal closed in 1859 and much of its course was filled in when the 'Sprat and Winkle' railway line was built in 1865. Much of this route now forms part of a long distance footpath, the Test Way.

In the second half of the nineteenth century a new form of transport imposed itself on the Hampshire landscape. The railways, requiring no more than gentle curves and gradients, cut swathes through the landscape. At the peak of the railway system no village in Hampshire could have been more than ten miles from a railway line. In addition to those still surviving today, there were lines along the valleys of the Test and the Meon linking respectively Southampton, Romsey and Andover, and Winchester, Alresford and Alton.

The Hampshire terrain is not difficult but even here the scale of works required to build the railways was staggering. For instance, on the London to Southampton line, engineered by Joseph Locke:

> "sixteen million cubic feet of earth were moved in making the cuttings and embankments, mostly between Basingstoke and Winchester: some of the most extensive cuttings in the world are on this stretch of line."[2]

The invention of the motor car had little immediate effect on the landscape, other than more strenuous efforts to improve the surface of the country's roads. The pace of road development has however accelerated during the twentieth century and, with the increasing size and volume of traffic and the necessity to move large amounts of freight, the impact has

become greater. The greatest impact has been made by the building of the motorways which bisect Hampshire. In a smaller but no less important way the development of by-passes, of which the Winchester by-pass, built in the 1930s, was one of the earliest in the country, has changed the look of the county.

As we have now seen, the biggest single influence on the shape of the landscape has been human. The countryside has been managed largely for the production of food and for commercial reasons. In contrast, the motivation behind the creation of landscaped parks and gardens was largely one of pleasure.

Nothing but archaeological evidence survives of the earliest gardens in Hampshire, such as those that were known to have existed at Romsey and Beaulieu Abbeys, but a medieval garden has been created in Queen Eleanor's Garden, to the rear of the Great Hall in Winchester. The sixteenth-century garden at Basing

Hillier Gardens and Arboretum

House, considered to be one of the most beautiful and well known of its day, is also being re-created.

During the eighteenth century, following the taste for Grand Tours to Italy and Greece, the gardens of the nobility were adapted to reflect classical taste, and the gardens of Hampshire still shelter many classical curiosities. Among the follies at Highclere Castle, for example, is 'Jackdaws Castle', which incorporates six classical columns from Berkeley House in London and is an eye catcher in the form of a classical temple at the end of a vista.

Later in the eighteenth century picturesque estate cottages replaced Gothic ruins and classical temples as objects of interest to be placed in the landscape. This style could even be adapted for principle residences, as can be seen in the cottage ornée built by Nash at the end of the eighteenth century, in a superb setting on the banks of the River Test at Houghton.

Many gardens created in the eighteenth and nineteenth centuries in Hampshire survive. One reason for this, and this is a common theme behind much of the history of the county, has been the continuing wealth of estate owners. The best known exponent of the landscaped garden was Lancelot 'Capability' Brown and the main surviving example of his work in Hampshire is Broadlands but he also worked on the landscape of Highclere Castle and Cadland, on Southampton Water.

From 1820 onwards Sir George Staunton, following his employment with the East India Company in China, created a landscaped garden in the eighteenth-century tradition at Leigh Park, Havant. He incorporated into the garden follies inspired by his travels and plants he brought back from the East. The taste for landscape gardening, rooted in the eighteenth century, developed into the nineteenth-century fashion for horticulture. A major contribution to this trend being the passion for collecting exotic plants from around the world, an increase in selective breeding and the creation of hybrids.

Hampshire was a particular centre for work on rhododendrons, especially at Highclere in the 1820s. The leading role of Hampshire gardens and gardeners continued with the work of William Wildsmith of Heckfield Place. Wildsmith was the most celebrated gardener of the late Victorian era. The firm of Hillier's was founded in 1854 by Edwin Hillier who had worked as a gardener at great houses such as Syon and Studley Royal. In 1953 his grandson, Sir Harold Hillier, founded the world famous collection of trees and shrubs, the Hillier Gardens and Arboretum, near Romsey. This collection includes over ten thousand species.

In the late nineteenth and early twentieth centuries there was a return to the integration of garden design with the architecture of the house. The best surviving example of this in Hampshire is the garden created by

Gertrude Jekyll for the house designed by Edwin Lutyens at Marshcourt near Stockbridge. The garden is an elaborate scheme of surrounding terraces, balustrades, walls and pergolas that complement the position of the house on a spur overlooking the Test Valley.

At Exbury a country house with a small park was built in the late eighteenth century for the Mitford family. In the 1920s and 1930s the Rothschild family used the garden and parkland to develop their world famous collection of rhododendrons and azaleas. The Exbury strain of azaleas is internationally famous and more than one thousand two hundred new hybrids have been created.

This brief survey of the gardens of Hampshire would not be complete without mentioning some of the smaller or specialist gardens which might not individually be considered significant to the landscape of Hampshire but added together form part of its rich fabric. Notable among

MOTTISFONT ABBEY GARDEN

The River Test

these are the riverside and rose gardens of Mottisfont Abbey; the gardens of Jenkyns Place, Bentley; and Macpenny's, Bransgore and Furzey Gardens in the New Forest.

Hampshire's estates and their owners' leisure pursuits have contributed to the look of the countryside in another significant way. In the late Victorian and Edwardian era belts of trees were planted along field edges, and hedgerows and small copses of trees were retained in order to provide shelter for game, especially pheasants and partridges for shooting.

Hampshire's rivers, in particular the Test, are famous for their fishing. Trout is the main attraction for the sportsman and the banks of the rivers are kept clear of vegetation. The fishing is considered to be so valuable that it would be damaged by public access and so few footpaths have been permitted along the banks.

The landscape of Hampshire has developed through a complex series of influences. Its geology and the climate have provided the raw materials but, as we have seen in this chapter, the countryside has been created by the way it has been used for thousands of years. An intricate collage and series of overlays make up what we see today. Each element, however insignificant, contributes to the whole picture. Of equal importance to this picture are the houses, villages, towns and cities of Hampshire.

Farley Chamberlayne Church

CHAPTER 3

ARCHITECTURE

Having had a chance to look at the landscape, what should the visitor without map or compass search for next? I would look for the nearest farm or village. After the landscape, it is domestic architecture, houses and farms, that provide the clearest guidance to which part of the country we are in.

Although building materials and housing types do obviously cross county boundaries, the particular mixture in any one county is likely to be unique, and vernacular architecture plays a major part in giving a region its individual character. The reason for this is that domestic buildings are usually constructed as easily as possible and, for much of history, this has necessitated the use of locally available materials.

For a county the size of Hampshire the geological picture is a surprisingly simple one with, as we saw in the last chapter, a broad band of chalk running through the centre of the county, and, to the north and south of it, gravels and clays. Naturally occurring stone was therefore limited principally to the flint found in chalk. Because of this lack of stone, other locally available materials had to be used. The most important of these were bricks which, until the coming of the canals and railways, were mainly made locally. Materials such as flint, timber and the less seen cob – compacted earth and clay – or clunch, a chalk based version of cob – could not be used on their own. Walls made of these needed strengthening, particularly at the corners, and here brick or stone were used.

The picture is further modified when we look at roof types. The predominant traditional material in Hampshire is thatch which, whilst its use mainly follows the chalk, is also used in the older traditional cottages of the New Forest. In the east of the county thatch gives way to tiles, a roofing material more usually seen in Sussex. It is interesting however to note that true cruck construction for the timber framing of cottages, common throughout the west country, does not extend over the eastern border of Hampshire into Surrey or Sussex.

The most commonly occurring small house type in Hampshire is the thatched, one-and-a-half-storeyed building, often called a 'bun-cottage'. With eyebrows of thatch over the half-dormers and the rounded outlines curving down over the half-hipped ends of the cottages, many of them look as if they have grown naturally. A variety of walling materials are used, the most common being flint and brick, or brick used with timber. An exception to the ubiquity of flint and brick can be found in and around Selborne where many of the houses are made from a local outcrop of pale cream malmstone together with bricks made of clay taken from between Oakhanger and Selborne.

Usually more substantial and rarely thatched, farmhouses follow a similar

continued on page 50

Thatched wall made of clunch

HAMPSHIRE 'BUN COTTAGE', ABBOTTS ANN

The Tithe Barn at Grange Farm, Basingstoke

continued from page 47

pattern, being most commonly built of brick or brick and flint. As far as farm buildings are concerned, the characteristic building type of the south-eastern farmstead is the large aisled barn, with steeply sloping roofs extending almost to the ground. In Hampshire these were usually built of timber and, when built for the great estates, could assume magnificent proportions. Among the best examples are the timber tithe barn at Titchfield Abbey, dating from the fifteenth century, and that at Basing House, built of brick in the sixteenth century, which reaches cathedral-like proportions.

In looking at individual houses, we should not ignore their grouping in villages. The setting of many villages in Hampshire, amongst fields and woods in the river valleys, or under beech hangers on the slopes of the chalk downs, are as fine as the villages themselves. An essential part of this landscape is the parish church.

Often little larger than houses, the

FARLEY CHAMBERLAYNE CHURCH

Winchester Cathedral

Medieval tiles in Winchester Cathedral

earliest churches, those built by the Saxons, were constructed of flint, timber or cob, and surviving examples can be seen in various places including Corhampton and Little Somborne. Although the Normans were to import stone, principally from the Isle of Wight and Caen, this was used only in cathedrals, castles and other important buildings. With a few notable exceptions, including East Meon, parish churches continued to be built, in the main, of locally available materials.

Flint, usually dressed with stone at the corners, and around the windows and doors, and timber used for the belfries, were the principal building materials used in Hampshire churches.

Timber steeples abound in the two counties of the old diocese of Winchester, Hampshire and Surrey, and are characteristic of it. In later centuries churches were also built of brick, often locally made. The Church of St Peter and St Paul, Fareham is notable for the extensive use made of local blue bricks dressed with 'Fareham reds'.

The Normans altered many Saxon churches and replaced others, including the Saxon minster which was at the heart of King Alfred's Winchester. Winchester Cathedral is:

> "... the most impressive display in England of architecture of the first generation after the Conquest." [1]

The present building retains its Norman framework, although it was added to in later periods, the nave in particular being altered in the fourteenth century.

In 1136 a grandson of William the Conqueror, Henry de Blois, then Bishop of Winchester, used part of his vast personal wealth to found St Cross Hospital. The Church of St Cross, which dominates the road into Winchester from the south, is a fine, largely Norman building. Inside, the tall round arches, with zig-zag decoration, give a great feeling of solidity. Henry de Blois also built Wolvesey Castle in Winchester at the time he made a bid for Winchester to become a seat for the Archbishopric. Wolvesey Castle became a ruin when it was slighted in the Civil War.

The other exceptionally fine Norman church in Hampshire is Romsey Abbey. Built with stone from Chilmark, it was first founded in 907 by Edward the Elder but was completely rebuilt between 1120 and 1230 and is surprisingly complete today. It owes this more than anything to having been bought to be used as a parish church by the people of the town at the time of the dissolution of the monasteries.

The Normans built their castles as an architectural expression of lordship and power. They were built to dominate rural settlements and towns and to control newly won land, river crossings, roads and valleys. Few of these survive in Hampshire although the remains of mottes can be seen near Southwick and at Rowner near Gosport. Finest among the military remains of the Norman period in Hampshire is Portchester Castle. The Castle, surrounded on three sides by the waters of Portsmouth Harbour, has a Norman keep rising from the outer walls of flint built by the Romans.

Portchester Castle dominates the approach from the sea and, towards the end of the twelfth century, and in the early part of the thirteenth century, it was important as a royal fortress, especially in connection with military manoeuvres and embarkations. In the succeeding centuries it was put to a variety of uses including a royal residence by Richard II and a prison during the Napoleonic Wars. A complete, stone built, Norman church nestles within the walls of the castle. The building of Portchester Castle was the beginning of Portsmouth Harbour's importance in Britain's naval heritage.

In the years following the Norman Conquest Hampshire was to become a centre for religious activity.

PORTCHESTER CASTLE

Monasteries were founded in the twelfth and thirteenth centuries, most notably at Netley, Titchfield and Beaulieu but also at Southwick, Selborne, Hamble and Ellingham. The Normans built up substantial wealth within little more than a century of their Conquest and this was to a great extent derived from their monastic estates. By the end of the thirteenth century, twenty-five per cent of land in Hampshire was owned by the Church. This wealth was used to finance the building of Winchester Cathedral and the art that adorns it.

The Castle at Winchester was built originally as a royal palace by Henry III between 1222 and 1236. The only part which survives intact, the Great Hall, is regarded as "the finest medieval hall in England, after Westminster Hall"[2]. For centuries it was used as a court. Sir Walter Raleigh was tried twice as a traitor in the Great Hall and Judge Jefferies held some of his notorious Bloody Assizes there. Most notable among those who were executed after their trial in the Great Hall in 1685 was Alice Lisle, who gave sanctuary in her home at Ringwood to fugitives from the unsuccessful rebellion against James II. Cleared of its temporary court room fittings when the new Law Courts were built next door in the 1970s, the Great Hall can now be seen in all its medieval glory. After the Law Courts were constructed, a set of fine stainless steel gates were made by Antony Robinson to close off the restored entrance between the two buildings.

At the dissolution of the monasteries the principal foundations and estates were put into the hands of the Crown and leading private individuals. In Hampshire, abbeys such as Beaulieu, Titchfield and Mottisfont were converted by their new owners into private houses, and this was a significant period for the development of the stately home. The rediscovery of brick around 1600 also did much to affect the appearance of the county. Bricks were to be used at an early stage of their development in the building of such great houses as Bramshill and The Vyne, near Basingstoke, built in the reign of Henry VIII of red brick, with a diaper pattern in dark bricks.

Most of the great houses in Hampshire were built for, or occupied at a significant point in their development by, owners who were major figures in the affairs of Britain. Hampshire's proximity to London was the main reason for the surprising number of these great houses. Thomas Wriothesley, Earl of Southampton, converted parts of Titchfield Abbey into a mansion soon after the Dissolution. Both Mottisfont Abbey, which came to him at the Dissolution, and The Vyne were owned by Lord Sandys, Lord Chamberlain from 1526 to 1540, for part of their history. Chaloner Chute, who became Speaker of the House of Commons, bought The Vyne in 1653.

Stratfield Saye was given by a grateful nation to the Duke of

THE VYNE, SHERBORNE ST JOHN

Highclere Castle

Wellington after the Battle of Waterloo. Broadlands, near Romsey, has been the home of both Lord Palmerston, Prime Minister from 1855 to 1861, and Lord Mountbatten. Built originally in the 1770s, Highclere Castle was completely remodelled by Sir Charles Barry, who also designed the Houses of Parliament, for the third Earl of Carnarvon in 1839–42. Highclere is the largest mansion in Hampshire.

Most notable in Hampshire among the dwellings designed by Edwin Lutyens, probably the last great architect of the country house, is Marshcourt, near Stockbridge. Built for the newly wealthy Herbert Johnson on a prominent position above the River Test, it was constructed from local materials, chalk ashlar with random bits of flint and tile. Lutyens was also responsible for New Place, Shedfield, built in 1906 entirely of deep red brick.

Hampshire's place at the centre of the south of England has meant that its coast has continued to be of great military and naval significance throughout its history. In addition to Portchester there are a string of fortifications along the coastline which mark the times when England has been threatened with invasion, or there has been a perceived threat.

Henry VIII built a number of forts along the coast in the 1540s to counter the threat of invasion and to defend the sheltered anchorages of the Solent. Hurst, Calshot, Netley and Southsea Castles were all built at this period. Calshot remains largely unaltered. Originally built in 1746, Fort Cumberland, in Portsmouth, was reconstructed in 1786 and is one of the finest surviving examples of an eighteenth-century star fortress.

By the end of the seventeenth century Portsmouth Dockyard had become the chief naval base in Britain but its development on a large and permanent scale began in the eighteenth century and the dockyard contains some of the finest military architecture in the country. In the middle of the nineteenth century a series of fifteen forts were built in a ring around Portsmouth. Built when Palmerston was Prime Minister, these forts, including those at Spithead, were constructed to prepare against the threat of French invasion.

Evidence of twentieth-century military activity abounds along the coast. The massive hangar on Calshot Spit was built to house the sea-planes which were pioneered on the Solent in the 1920s. Evidence of the preparations for the D-Day landings of 1944 can be seen at Lepe and on Hayling Island, where sections for the Mulberry Harbours were made. In the north of the county, in Aldershot, the home of the British Army, there are again some fine examples of military architecture, most notably Prince Consort's Library, built in 1860.

Earlier we looked at the setting of villages in the landscape. Townscapes can be equally characteristic of a region and the typical town in

Broad Street, New Alresford

Hampshire has a broad street lined with houses, many of them built of brick. Good examples can be seen at Wickham, Alton, Alresford and Odiham. New Alresford was founded in 1199 by Bishop de Lucy of Winchester. Most of the medieval houses in Broad Street were destroyed by fires in 1689 and 1736 but their replacements are good seventeenth- and eighteenth-century buildings.

It is not just the buildings themselves which reflect the character of a region. The quantity and quality of the decoration can give a powerful impression of its wealth at various periods in history. The integration of art and architecture reached its finest expression in the work of medieval craftsmen, and the cathedrals built, re-built and embellished in the three hundred years after the Norman Conquest are the finest memorials to their workmanship. However, in England, it was the Saxons who first integrated art into their architecture.

As we have seen, few Saxon

Tournai marble font, East Meon

churches remained unaltered after the Norman Conquest and, because of this, the amount of Saxon sculpture that has survived anywhere is rare. It is in this context that the Saxon sculpture in Hampshire is important:

> "Stone sculpture on a large scale up to the early eleventh century is a great rarity on the Continent as well as in England. The Hampshire group is perhaps the most important anywhere."[3]

Particularly important, and best preserved, is the Romsey Rood. Also significant in assessing the worth of Saxon sculpture, although they only exist as shadows, are the Crucifixion groups with the Virgin and St John at Headbourne Worthy and Breamore. Other existing works include a tombstone at Whitchurch, part of a stone cross at Steventon, sundials with leaf decoration at Corhampton and Warnford, and wall paintings at Nether Wallop.

With the arrival of the Normans, styles changed dramatically. This is well illustrated by the change from the softness of the Romsey Rood to the resolutely organized yet lively figures of the Tournai Fonts. Only ten of these fonts, made from Tournai marble, exist in England, four of them in Hampshire – in Winchester Cathedral and in the churches at East Meon, St Michael's, Southampton and St Mary Bourne.

Probably the best example in Hampshire of the art of the Norman stonemason can be seen in the capitals from columns in Hyde Abbey. Now on display in St Bartholomew's Church, Hyde, in Winchester, these have the typical vigour, simplicity and formality, of early twelfth-century craftsmanship. By the early thirteenth century, styles appear to have adopted a greater realism, as can be seen in the figure of Ecclesia, carved in 1230, and described by Pevsner as the "finest piece of its date in England". This now stands in the retro-choir aisle of Winchester Cathedral.

Winchester Cathedral contains many outstanding works of art and craftsmanship. In the Chapel of the Holy Sepulchre and the Chapel of the Guardian Angels are some of the best thirteenth-century wall paintings in England, and in the Lady Chapel there is a wall painting dating from the early sixteenth century. The Pilgrim Gates, believed to be 800 years old, are the oldest wrought iron grill work in England. The misericords of the fourteenth century have varied and fine carving, and among the modern commissions are two new misericords by Susan Wraight.

At one time the majority of churches would have been decorated with wall paintings but the whitewash of reformers and the passage of time has removed or dimmed all but a few. However, important fourteenth-century wall paintings can be seen at Idsworth, in the south east of the county, and at Hurstbourne Tarrant where 'The Quick and the Dead' and 'The Wheel of Fortune' are portrayed. The wooden painted reredos in Romsey Abbey is an uncommon

Fourteenth-century wall paintings, Idsworth

survival of the early sixteenth century.

The richness, and sometimes the quality, of funerary monuments in churches is usually another expression of the wealth of an area, and in Hampshire there are many fine examples. William of Wykeham's marble memorial in Winchester Cathedral is a good early example of the move away from the stereotyped tomb figures of which there are several in the Cathedral.

The Wriothesley Monument in Titchfield Church, erected early in the seventeenth century, is reputed to be one of the finest alabaster and marble monuments in Britain. It was paid for by the second Earl of Southampton and executed by Gerard Johnson, an exiled Flemish sculptor living in London. Neo-classicism is represented in church monuments by the memorial to Charlotte Chamberlayne in Jesus Chapel, Peartree Green. Carved by Sir Francis Chantry in 1835, this is a moving and romantic memorial showing the delicacy of

The Guildhall, Portsmouth

FILLING WATER BOTTLES, *A SECTION OF THE PAINTINGS BY STANLEY SPENCER IN SANDHAM MEMORIAL CHAPEL, BURGHCLERE*

marble carving to good effect. Fine examples continue into the twentieth century, notably the memorial by Fuchs to Mrs Ashley in Romsey Abbey carved in marble in 1913.

Whilst the incorporation of art into architecture never entirely died out, Hampshire had to wait until the second half of the nineteenth century for significant works to be created in its churches; for example, a fresco by Lord Leighton under the east window of the Victorian Church of St Michael and All Angels in Lyndhurst painted in 1864. In 1893, the artist Heywood Sumner carried out sgraffito decoration over the chancel arcades in Christ Church, Church Crookham. In 1901 he also executed the now restored sgraffito murals in St Agatha's Church, Portsmouth, using the same technique.

The integration of art and architecture has continued in the twentieth century. Most notable are the paintings by Stanley Spencer in the Sandham Memorial Chapel, at

The Whistler Room, Mottisfont Abbey
(Photo: copyright National Trust, 1991)

Burghclere, which were commissioned as a memorial to Lieut. H.W. Sandham, who died in 1919 from an illness contracted in the war in Macedonia. The chapel was designed by Lionel Pearson to allow Spencer to complete a cycle of paintings portraying war service in Salonika. This was his memorial to those who died in the First World War. British art was not in the mainstream of European developments at the time but Spencer's work was wholly original and has been described as England's prime contribution to European Expressionism.

Equally fine in its own way is the decoration by Rex Whistler of the drawing room at Mottisfont Abbey completed in 1939. This is an accomplished example of trompe-l'oeil decoration. Simple Gothic decoration blends well with the literal portrayal of the smoking urn, draped with an ermine stole and on a base heaped with books, and the small paint pot, brush and box of matches, apparently carelessly left on the feigned cornice.

A less well-known example of the mural tradition, but one which gives the viewer a real feeling for place, can be seen on the walls of Woodgreen Village Hall. Painted by two students of the Royal College of Art, Robert Baker and Edward Payne, in the 1930s, it covers the walls of the main hall and portrays over seventy residents of the village in scenes of rural life.

The character of the area and a sense of place are also caught in the etched glass windows by Lawrence Whistler, at Steep in memory of Edward Thomas, at Ashmansworth in memory of the composer Gerald Finzi, and at Hannington. Individuality is given to All Saints Church in Basingstoke by the three windows designed by Cecil Collins and made by Patrick Reyntiens, and to St Marks Church, Kempshott, by the altar and high chairs made by Richard La Trobe Bateman in 1987.

This chapter on the architecture of Hampshire started with the humble domestic dwellings, farms and villages which help to define the character of Hampshire. But it is not only vernacular architecture which gives the county its individuality; it is also those buildings of national importance such as Winchester Cathedral and Portchester Castle; the great houses which owe their creation and retention to the significant number of powerful and wealthy people who have lived in Hampshire; the fortifications and naval architecture of Portsmouth; and the prolific amount of art which adorns Hampshire's architecture. In themselves these may not be unique to the county but they are often the finest examples of their type and collectively contribute to the rich fabric of Hampshire.

Fields near Morestead

CHAPTER 4

LITERATURE

"IN THE SOUTH, woods upon the hills are dissolving into a deep blue smoke, without form except at their upper edges. And in the north and north-west the high lands of Berkshire and Wiltshire are prostrate and violet through thirty miles of witching air. That also is a call to go on and on and over St Catherine's Hill and through Winchester until the brain is drowsed with the colours of night and day."

So the poet Edward Thomas, standing on the Downs in the east of the county, portrayed Hampshire. Many writers have described the Hampshire landscape, or set their works here, but Edward Thomas, although not born in the county, is probably the most 'Hampshire' of writers, with the countryside he loved imbuing the fabric of his work.

Throughout history, just as human influence has changed the landscape, so artists have drawn inspiration from it. They have recorded their surroundings and significant events that have taken place there; musicians have tried to capture the quintessential essence of the landscape; writers have written about or set their books in it. Any study of the sense of place must include the artist's response to it and in the next two chapters we will be looking at some of this work.

The elements of the Hampshire landscape that have inspired writers and painters most have been those things that help to define its individuality. So the downs, river valleys and the sea are the main recurring themes.

One of the earliest references in poetry to Hampshire is by Michael Drayton who, in 1612, wrote of the Solent:

"Where those rough irefull Tides, as in her Straits they meet,
With boystrous shocks and rores each other rudely greet,
Which fiercelie when they charge, and sadlie make retreat,
Upon the bulwarkt Forts of Hurst and Calshot beat"[1]

William Shakespeare was a visitor in the 1590s to Titchfield Abbey which had, after the dissolution of the monasteries, been rebuilt by Thomas Wriothesley, first Earl of Southampton. It is thought that Shakespeare may have written some of his poetry, including a number of his sonnets, whilst staying at the Abbey as well as *Love's Labour's Lost.* Together with *Romeo and Juliet* and *A Midsummer Night's Dream*, these plays may have been given their first performances in the Earl's Great Hall.

Several writers have recorded journeys through Hampshire in their diaries and travellers have written about the county. In the latter part of the seventeenth century Celia Fiennes, one of the most intrepid travellers of her day, recorded her visits to Hampshire. Her writings may contain little detail about the landscape but they are interesting for the descriptions of the towns and places she stayed in and the great houses she passed.

Daniel Defoe, writing in the 1720s, described Hampshire as "one of the best wooded counties in Britain". On his second journey through Britain, Defoe visited the sea coasts of Kent, Sussex and Hampshire, before returning to London. Arriving in Portsmouth he saw:

"the largest fortification, beyond comparison, that we have in England. The situation of this place is such, that it is chosen ... for the best security to the navy above all the places in Britain; the entrance into the harbour is safe, but very narrow, guarded on both sides by terrible platforms of cannon particularly on the point."[2]

On his third journey Defoe returned to Hampshire and visited Winchester. On leaving the town, travelling south westwards, he came:

"... to the most charming plains, and most pleasant country of that kind in England; which continues, with very small intersections of rivers and valleys, for above fifty miles ..."[3]

Perhaps the traveller who most

TITCHFIELD ABBEY

closely observed the countryside of Hampshire was William Cobbett. Born in Surrey, Cobbett lived for a time in the early years of the nineteenth century in Hampshire. In his introduction to the Penguin edition of *Rural Rides* George Woodcock says:

"Few writers have been more passionately involved in their daily thoughts with the rural life of England. Few have described more evocatively, or for that matter, more accurately, the beauties of that England south of the Thames to which Cobbett belonged by emotional loyalty."

In a classic passage Cobbett compares the landscape around Winchester with his native Surrey and Kent and concludes that:

"There are not many finer spots in England; and if I were to take in a circle of eight or ten miles of semi-diameter, I should say that I believe there is not one so fine. Here are hill, dell, water, meadows, woods, corn-fields, downs; and all of them very fine and beautifully disposed... As a spot to live on (I like nothing more than) a country where high downs prevail, with here and there a large wood on the top or side of a hill, and where you see, in the deep dells, here and there a farmhouse, and here or there a village, the buildings sheltered by a group of lofty trees."

When visiting east Hampshire, Cobbett was struck by the beauty of the beech hangers:

"We came, all in a moment, at the very edge of the hanger! And, never, in all my life, was I so surprised and so delighted! I pulled up my horse, and sat and looked; and it was like looking from the top of a castle down into the sea, except that the valley was land and not water... Those who had so strenuously dwelt on the dirt and dangers of this route, had said not a word about the beauties, the matchless beauties of the scenery."

These characteristic beech hangers were also part of Edward Thomas's Hampshire:

"They are steep-sided bays, running and narrowing far into and up the sides of the chalk hills and especially of those hills with which the high flinty plateau breaks down to the greensand and the plain. These steep sides are clothed with beeches, thousands of beeches interrupted by the black yews which resemble caverns among the paler trees, or, in the spring, by the green haze of a few larches and the white flames of the beam tree buds."[4]

B. B., author of *Brendon Chase* and *Little Grey Men*, was another writer to comment on the beech hangers when he visited Selborne on his *White Road Westwards* in the 1950s. On his visit he climbed the 'Zig-Zag' path which had been made by the Reverend Gilbert White in the eighteenth century.

Gilbert White, author of *The Natural History and Antiquities of Selborne*, was already well known by the time Cobbett made a special visit to Selborne on one of his *Rural Rides* in 1823.

Principally a pioneering natural historian, Gilbert White, born in 1720 in Selborne, where he died seventy-three years later, did describe his beloved village in verse:

THE 'ZIG-ZAG', SELBORNE

"Now climb the steep, drop now your eye below,
Where round the blooming village orchards grow;
There, like a picture, lies my lowly seat,
A rural, shelter'd, unobserv'd retreat.
Me far above the rest Selbornian scenes,
The pendant forests, and the mountain greens
Strike with delight; there spreads the distant view,
That gradual fades till sunk in misty blue."

In 1903 W. H. Hudson, author of *A Shepherd's Life* and *Far Away and Long Ago*, published *Hampshire Days*. Gilbert White and W. H. Hudson are probably England's greatest nature writers and *Hampshire Days*, whilst less well known, stands alongside *The Natural History of Selborne* as a classic of nature writing. These two works, together with the poems of Edward Thomas, can, I think, be said to be Hampshire's gift to English literature because they draw their inspiration from Hampshire and are completely steeped in its nature and landscape.

Hudson made several visits to Selborne:

"the best of Selborne is the common on the hill – all the better for the steep hill which must be climbed to get to it... This hill-top common is the most forest-like, the wildest in England, and the most beautiful as well, both in its trees and tangles of all kinds of wild plants that flourish in waste places, and in the prospects which one gets of the surrounding country."

Much of *Hampshire Days* is devoted to the natural history of the New Forest but Hudson did travel throughout the county; for example:

"There are no more refreshing places in Hampshire, one might almost say in England, than the green level valleys of the Test and Itchen that wind, alternately widening and narrowing, through the downland country to Southampton Water."

Jane Austen is by far and away the best known Hampshire writer. Born in Steventon in 1775, she died in Winchester in 1817 and is buried in the Cathedral. She lived thirty-seven of her forty-two years in the county, in Steventon, Southampton, Chawton and Winchester. Yet for all this long association with Hampshire she did not write about the county, with one exception, in an identifiable way. Maggie Lane in *Jane Austen's England* says:

"I believe that Jane Austen deliberately avoided, out of respect for her acquaintance and fear of identification, using her beloved Hampshire countryside as the setting for a novel... Surrey took its place when she came to describe her ideal community (in *Emma*)."[5]

The one exception is in *Mansfield Park* where she describes a walk taken by the Price family on the ramparts of Old Portsmouth after attending service at the Garrison Church:

"The day was uncommonly lovely. It was really March; but it was April in its mild air, brisk soft wind, and bright sun, occasionally clouded for a minute; and every thing looked so beautiful under the influence of such a sky, the effects of the

Jane Austen's House, Chawton

GOSPORT (ENTRANCE TO PORTSMOUTH HARBOUR)
c 1830, J.M.W. TURNER (PRIVATE COLLECTION)

shadows pursuing each other, on the ships at Spithead and the island beyond, with the ever-varying hues of the sea now at high water, dancing in its glee and dashing against the ramparts with so fine a sound, produced altogether such a combination of charms for Fanny, as made her gradually almost careless of the circumstances under which she felt them."

The late summer of 1819 found the poet John Keats in Winchester. In a letter to a friend he wrote:

"How beautiful the season is now – How fine the air. A temperate sharpness about it... I never lik'd stubble-fields so much as now – Aye better than the chilly green of the Spring. Somehow a stubble-plain looks warm – in the same way that some pictures look warm – This struck me so much in my Sunday's walk that I composed upon it."

What he wrote is thought to be the *Ode to Autumn*, which begins:

"Season of mists and mellow fruitfulness!
Close bosom-friend of the maturing sun;
Conspiring with him how to load and
bless

With fruit the vines that round the thatch-eaves run;
To bend with apples the mossed cottage-trees,
And fill all fruit with ripeness to the core;
To swell the gourd, and plump the hazel shells
With a sweet kernel; to set budding more,
And still more, later flowers for the bees,
Until they think warm days will never cease,
For summer has o'er-brimmed their clammy cells."

Charles Dickens was born in Portsmouth but his family left when he was only two. However he did return to gather local atmosphere for *Nicholas Nickleby*. Nicholas meets Vincent Crummles on the Portsmouth road and he and Smike join his theatre company for their season in the city. On their journey from London, Dickens describes the scene before Nicholas and Smike reach the inn twelve miles north of Portsmouth where he meets Crummles:

"Onward they kept, with steady purpose, and entered at length upon a wide and spacious tract of downs, with every variety of little hill and plain to change their verdant surface. Here, there shot up, almost perpendicularly, into the sky, a height so steep, as to hardly be accessible to any but the sheep and goats that fed upon its sides, and there, stood a mound of green, sloping and tapering off so delicately, and merging so gently into the level ground, that you could scarce define its limits. Hills swelling above each other; and undulations, shapely and uncouth, smooth and rugged, graceful and grotesque, thrown negligently side by side, bounded the view in each direction... By degrees, the prospect receded more and more on either hand, and as they had been shut out from rich and extensive scenery, so they emerged once again upon the open country."

Other writers to have written about Portsmouth, or with connections to the city, include Rudyard Kipling, whose characters visited Southsea in *The Light That Failed*, and H. G. Wells, who described in *Kipps* the misery of his apprenticeship at Hyde's Drapery Establishment in Kings Road, Southsea. Conan Doyle conceived Sherlock Holmes whilst he was practising as a doctor in Portsmouth. One of the adventures of Sherlock Holmes, *The Copper Beeches*, is set in and around Winchester.

The model for the hospital in Trollope's *The Warden* is St Cross in Winchester but a map of Trollope's Barsetshire, and he did draw one, might be imposed on any part of southern England. Thomas Hardy's Wessex, on the other hand, is far more specific. In *Tess of the D'Urbervilles*, Tess is hung in Wintoncester (Winchester) Gaol and Angel Clare and his sister-in-law leave the city by the Westgate as the execution is carried out:

"When they had nearly reached the top of the great West Hill the clocks in the town struck eight. Each gave a start at the notes, and, walking onward yet a few steps, they reached the first milestone, standing

Butser Hill

Fields near Droxford, Meon Valley

whitely on the green margin of the grass, and backed by the down, which here was open to the road... The prospect from the summit was almost unlimited. In the valley beneath lay the city they had just left, its more prominent buildings showing as in an isometric drawing – among them the broad cathedral tower, with its Norman windows and immense length of aisle and nave, the spires of St Thomas's, the pinnacled tower of the College, and, more to the right, the tower and gables of the ancient hospice, where to this day the pilgrim may receive his dole of bread and ale. Behind the city swept the rotund upland of St Catherine's Hill; further off, landscape beyond landscape, till the horizon was lost in the radiance of the sun hanging above it."

The writer I most associate with Hampshire is Edward Thomas, who lived near Petersfield from 1906 until he went to France, where he was killed on the battlefield at Arras in 1917. Hampshire, particularly the area around his home, along with the shadow of the Great War, which

Tower, Gatehouse, Winchester; drawn by W. H. Bartlett, figures by T. Baynes; etched by J. Le Keux

lengthened over his later poems, permeates all his poetry, and much of his later prose writing. So we get direct references in poems such as *The Lane*:

"Some day, I think, there will be people enough
In Froxfield to pick all the blackberries
Out of the hedges of Green Lane, the straight
Broad Lane where now September hides herself
In bracken and blackberry, harebell and dwarf gorse."

Or in his poem *May 23*:

"So off went Jack with his roll-walk-run,
Leaving his cresses from Oakshott rill
And his cowslips from Wheatham hill."

One of his longer poems describes the history of the inn, set *Up in The Wind* down a track on the downs of south-east Hampshire, whose sign to this day hangs empty as it did when Thomas described it:

"The post and empty frame
I knew. Without them I could not have guessed

Published by Longman and Co. for Britton's 'Picturesque Antiquities of English Cities'

The low grey house and its one stack
under trees
Was not a hermitage but a public-house".

Other twentieth-century poets who have written about places in Hampshire include John Betjeman who, as well as writing about Miss J. Hunter Dunn being "Furnish'd and burnished by Aldershot sun", wrote of *Youth and Age on Beaulieu River*:

"Early sun on Beaulieu water
Lights the underside of oaks,
Clumps of leaves it floods and blanches.
All transparent grow the branches
Which the double sunlight soaks;
To her craft on Beaulieu water
Clemency the General's daughter
Pulls across with even strokes."

Laurie Lee wrote of Southampton in his autobiographical novel *As I Walked Out One Midsummer Morning*:

"After a week on the road I finally arrived at Southampton, where I'd been told I would see the sea. Instead, I saw a few rusty cranes and a compressed looking liner wedged tightly between some houses; also some sad allotments fringing a muddy river which they said was Southampton Water.

"Southampton Town, on the other hand, came up to all expectations, proving to be salty and shifty in turns, like some ship-jumping sailor who'd turned his back on the sea in a desperate attempt to make good on land."

Later, when he left Southampton travelling eastwards, he wrote:

"A few miles from Southampton I saw the real sea at last, head on, a sudden end to a lane, a great sweep of curved nothing rolling out to the invisible horizon and revealing more distance than I'd ever seen before. It was green, and heaved gently like the skin of a frog, and carried drowsy little ships like flies. Compared with the land, it appeared to be a huge hypnotic blank, putting everything to sleep that touched it."

A number of the scenes described by Flora Thompson in a series of articles she wrote for a weekly magazine, the *Catholic Fireside*, in the 1920s were to reappear in the *Lark Rise to Candleford* trilogy. Flora Thompson lived in Hampshire for five years when her husband was postmaster at Liphook. Her love of the countryside of the borders of Hampshire and Surrey comes through in every word of these lyrical notes on nature and country life:

"To no part of England does spring come with more enchanting loveliness than to these secluded valleys beneath the southern hills...The heath and the hill, so dark and shaggy until a week ago, have burst into a conflagration of blossoming gorse; the water meadows are gilded with dandelion and kingcup, and the garden fruit trees stand snowy against the April blue of the sky."[6]

John Arlott, Hampshire man, cricket commentator, raconteur and poet, who died in 1992, was born in Basingstoke. Writing in 1943, under the pseudonym of Leslie Thomas, he described the town in a way Basingstoke's residents are unlikely to have approved of:

"Of Basingstoke in Hampshire
The claims to fame are small:–

The Empty Sign of the 'Pub With No Name'

The White Horse, or the 'Pub With No Name', Priors Dean

A derelict canal
And a cream and green Town Hall.
At each week-end the 'locals'
Line the Market Square,
And as the traffic passes,
They stand and stand and stare."

Hampshire places appear in the work of several novelists of the second half of the twentieth century. The hero of Neville Shute's novel *No Highway* worked at the Royal Aircraft Establishment at Farnborough, and much of *Requiem for a Wren* is concerned with the preparations for the D-Day landings in and around the Solent. Olivia Manning set her novel *The Play Room* in and around Portsmouth.

One of the most successful of post-war children's books, *Watership Down*, takes its name from a piece of the North Hampshire Downs. All the places in this novel are clearly identifiable and the author, Richard Adams, included a map of the area in the book so that the journeyings of the rabbit heroes could be followed.

"It was evening of the following day. The north-facing escarpment of Watership Down, in shadow since early morning, now caught the western sun for an hour before twilight. Three hundred feet the down rose vertically in a stretch of no more than six hundred – a precipitous wall, from the thin belt of trees at the foot to the ridge where the steep flattened out. The light, full and smooth, lay like a gold rind over the turf, the furze and yew bushes, the few wind-stunted thorn trees. From the ridge, the light seemed to cover all the slope below, drowsy and still."

On their travels the rabbits also cross the River Test:

"He remembered the Enborne, its surface broken by gravel spits and plant growth. The Test, a weed-cut, carefully tended trout stream, seemed to him like a world of water. A good ten yards wide it was, fast-flowing and smooth, spangling and dazzling in the evening sun. The tree-reflections on the even current were unbroken as on a lake. There was not a reed or plant to be seen above the water... The water was very clear, with a bed of clean, yellow gravel, and even in the middle was hardly four feet deep."

It may seem strange to end this chapter on literature inspired by Hampshire with a rabbit looking from a bridge into the River Test but it seems right to do so because the downland landscape of which Watership Down is a part is so much the landscape of Hampshire. It has formed a backdrop to the travels of Celia Fiennes, Defoe and Cobbett, has been the subject of detailed examination by Gilbert White and W. H. Hudson, has inspired poetry by Edward Thomas and John Betjeman and has featured in the novels of Dickens and Hardy, among others. The river valleys of central Hampshire, the cities of Portsmouth and Southampton, the New Forest and the waters of the Solent are also well represented – these are the landscapes which have featured in the work of so many writers reflecting the unique variety of Hampshire.

NOCTURNE IN BLACK AND GOLD: ENTRANCE TO SOUTHAMPTON WATER
BY JAMES MCNEILL WHISTLER (OIL ON CANVAS) (ART INSTITUTE OF CHICAGO)

CHAPTER 5

ART & MUSIC

THE STORY OF ART in Hampshire whilst involving, for the most part, less well known names than that of literature, does reveal some famous visitors and significant events in the history of English art. The account of its music will take less space to tell.

The history of art in Hampshire begins in Anglo-Saxon England. Once Alfred had secured his kingdom against the Vikings, he launched a substantial programme of educational and cultural revival. The charter which Edgar granted in 966 to the reformed monastery of New Minster, Winchester, was presented in the form of a book. Written in gold script and embellished with an elaborate frontispiece this work is one of the masterpieces of Saxon art and was created in Winchester.

Within half a century of the Norman Conquest, Henry de Blois, Bishop of Winchester, had brought a team of artists to Winchester to work on what was to become known as the Winchester Bible. The contents of this bible, one of a series of magnificent bibles produced during the twelfth century, illustrates the development of art at this period, and synthesizes the work of different schools. It includes the work of the earliest masters with centuries of artistic tradition behind them, with echoes of Anglo-Saxon art, Irish and Byzantine details, through to the flowing lines and pools of pattern by monks such as the so-called 'Master of the Gothic Majesty'.

Henry de Blois travelled throughout Europe and it is thought that artists from Winchester would have been in his entourage, thus subjecting them to influences from elsewhere in the Norman world, including Byzantium. Artists travelled from one monastery to another, although some artists remained in Winchester for the whole of their career. The 'Master of the Leaping Figures' may have been one such artist.

On the whole it is only the manuscripts of this period that have survived. From them, however, it is possible to envisage what Anglo-Saxon and Anglo-Norman art looked like. Larger works, for example wall paintings, have in the main been destroyed, damaged, or deteriorated. A few examples of other art and craft from this period do survive, such as the Winchester plaque which shows a representation of the Last Judgement and was made in Winchester in the middle of the twelfth century with remarkable virtuosity.

As we saw in the third chapter, art was closely linked to architecture throughout the medieval period and for some time afterwards. Even where landscape was shown in paintings it was usually a mythical and rarely a recognizable one. The popularity of topographical pictures grew in the seventeenth and eighteenth centuries and many pictures of places in Hampshire were made at this period.

In the late eighteenth century William Gilpin was appointed vicar of

NETLEY ABBEY

Boldre, in the New Forest. An artist himself, his books and essays on art were influential in formulating ideas on the 'natural' rendering of 'picturesque' landscape, as opposed to idealized 'classical' interpretations. Gilpin's writings were to influence a number of artists including the young Turner.

Gilpin drew his inspiration from the landscape and trees of the New Forest, which he spent a great deal of time exploring, drawing, and commenting on. Painters of the 'picturesque' drew inspiration from the landscape but sought variety, curious details and interesting textures, trees of a certain form and medieval ruins, which were quintessentially 'picturesque'.

Netley Abbey was the most painted subject in Hampshire in the late eighteenth and nineteenth centuries. This clearly illustrates the influence of the 'picturesque' at the time because the ruins of the Abbey were an ideal subject. Among the artists who painted there were Michael Angelo Rooker, Samuel Prout and Francis Towne. Towne's watercolour painted in 1798 is a typical example blending the ruins with simply articulated trees in an "almost claustrophobic intimacy"[1]

J. M. W. Turner visited Hampshire on a number of occasions. On his first visit in 1796 he painted in Winchester. He made several more visits in the 1820s, painting a number of watercolours to be published in two volumes of pictures of *Picturesque Views* and in *Ports of England*. Turner also executed marine paintings of ships in the Solent.

Broadly a contemporary of Turner, John Linnell travelled to Southampton on a number of occasions to draw from the landscape and to undertake commissions. The subject matter of his paintings grew out of the 'picturesque'. His landscapes of Hampshire are clearly located, but omit the detail of topographical works. Amongst others he painted pictures of the Itchen Ferry, Southampton Water, Lymington Quay and Netley Abbey.

Along with J. M. W. Turner, John Constable is Britain's best known landscape painter. He was unique in concentrating exclusively on the landscape of East Anglia and the work he did elsewhere was comparatively incidental and made on personal visits. After he married, in 1816, Constable and his wife, Maria, set off for Dorset by a leisurely route. Stopping in Southampton, probably to visit Netley Abbey, he executed a sketch, now in Southampton Art Gallery, of Town Quay and the anchorage, looking westward along the shore, showing Hythe in the background.

William Shayer Senior is one of the few artists who can genuinely be termed a 'Hampshire artist'. Not just because he was born in Southampton, in 1787, but because his principal love as a painter was the Hampshire countryside. This, except for spells as

THE VILLAGE FESTIVAL *BY WILLIAM SHAYER (OIL ON CANVAS) (TATE GALLERY, LONDON)*

THE FERRY, ITCHEN *BY JOHN LINNELL (1792–1882); OIL ON CANVAS, 1825*

St Catherine's Hill
by Heywood Sumner (etching)

a coach painter in Guildford and Chichester, kept him in Southampton and probably prevented him from becoming better known. His pictures tend not to be precise in location, although his *Sand-diggers in the New Forest* is clearly placed by the inclusion of the Rufus Stone. He showed great skill in his portrayal of figures in the landscape. This can be best appreciated in his painting *The Village Festival* which was composed from sketches made at Alverstoke.

Hampshire's seascapes, particularly Portsmouth and Spithead, attracted artists in the eighteenth and nineteenth centuries. Mention has already been made of Turner's visits. Others to have painted there include Dominic Serres and William Adolphus Knell. Being present, however, did not seem to be essential. John Cleveley the Younger, for example, painted his picture of the Spithead Review of 1773 without having been there. Many of the works of this period are monumental, either in size or purpose, as, for example, Henry Dawson's exhibit in the Royal Academy exhibition of 1866 which portrayed Southampton Water, Calshot Castle and the Isle of Wight. James Tissot, perhaps best known for his painting *The Captain's Daughter*, set two of his paintings in 1877 in Portsmouth. The second of these, *The Gallery of HMS Calcutta*, was "the last and most brilliant of his shipboard scenes" and, in common with many of the others, portrays a young man talking to a beautiful woman having retired from a ball on board ship.

In the 1860s and 1870s James McNeill Whistler twice visited Southampton and stayed with Sir Thomas Sutherland, Chairman of the Peninsular and Orient Line. This was at the time Whistler was painting his controversial series of Nocturnes. The first, *Nocturne: The Solent*, one of the early pictures in the series, shows ships at night on a calm sea with the land barely visible in the background. The second, *Nocturne in Black and Gold: Entrance to Southampton Water*, whilst equally minimal in the elements shown – sea, ships, full moon, and a faint trace of the shoreline – clearly evokes the entrance to one of the great harbours of the world.

Heywood Sumner was born in Alresford in 1853. As well as a muralist and designer of stained glass and wallpapers, he was a painter and illustrator, and one of the less well known members of the Arts and Crafts movement. He was among several artists to be inspired by the Itchen Valley, which was the subject matter of his earliest work, published in 1881. After a busy career in London he retired to the New Forest in 1904. Here he was to produce a lyrical series of watercolours, the design for a tapestry, *The Chace*, which is a romantic portrayal of the New Forest, and *The Book of Gorley*, a personal journal of his way of life which included anecdotes and illustrations of the people and history of the New Forest.

W. H. Allen was, at the turn of the century, Director of the Farnham School of Art, and during this time produced several thousand watercolours recording the landscape and farming of the border area between North Hampshire and Surrey. Not only are his pictures a unique record of a way of life that was disappearing but many of them are excellent works in their own right.

Hampshire has not provided the inspiration to artists of the twentieth century that other parts of the country such as Cornwall or Wales have, and there is certainly no equivalent of the St Ives School. Even artists who have drawn much of their inspiration from the landscape of the south of England, such as Paul Nash, Stanley Spencer and John Piper, did not execute many works in Hampshire. However each of these, and several other important artists of the twentieth century, have produced works of places in the county.

Sir Alfred Munnings (1878–1959)

A LAND GIRL AND THE BAIL BULL *BY EVELYN DUNBAR*
(OIL ON CANVAS) (TATE GALLERY, LONDON)

was primarily known as a painter of English country life. In 1911 he had set up a studio in Lamorna, Cornwall. It was from here that Munnings made his expeditions to Hampshire where, in 1913, he had discovered in the Gypsy hop-pickers a wealth of models. Munnings was to write of his visits:

"Of all my painting experiences, none were so alluring and colourful as those visits spent amongst the Gypsy hop-pickers in Hampshire each September."

Probably the most evocative of these works is *Gypsy Life: The Hop Pickers*, painted in 1913 near Alton.

The war-time 'Recording Britain' project produced forty-seven paintings of Hampshire. With the expectation of large scale destruction during the war, and in the light of pre-war developments in the countryside, the project used ninety-seven artists to record thirty-two English and four Welsh counties, beginning with the coastal counties, in over fifteen hundred works. Best known of the artists who worked in Hampshire

LOADING TIMBER, SOUTHAMPTON DOCKS *BY CHRISTOPHER NEVINSON (OIL ON CANVAS) (SOUTHAMPTON ART GALLERY)*

THE BATHERS *BY SAM SMITH (WOOD, PAINT, STRING)* (SOUTHAMPTON ART GALLERY)

were George Bissill, Raymond T. Cowern, and Thomas Hennell, who among other things, painted *The Beech Avenue, Lasham.*

Evelyn Dunbar worked in Hampshire as an Official War Artist. She concentrated on women's activities, particularly the Land Army. One of her works, *A Land Girl and the Bail Bull*, shows a Land Girl about to tether a bull among an outdoor dairy herd on the Hampshire Downs, a practice that has long since disappeared from the countryside.

Southampton has been portrayed in a number of works in the twentieth century. Christopher Nevinson, a leading British 'futurist' painter, painted a picture of timber being loaded in Southampton Docks in 1916/17. In 1956 L. S. Lowry painted *The Floating Bridge*, which used to be the main crossing over the Itchen River in Southampton.

Sam Smith was born in Southampton in 1908. Much of his work as an illustrator, sculptor, and maker of automata was inspired by the city and its port which thrived throughout the first half of the twentieth century. After art school he began work as an illustrator but it was when he began to make small wooden painted toys for a craft gallery in London that he found his true vocation, and he continued to produce these throughout the 1950s and 1960s – the majority of these were of small boats which,

> "were not models, but personifications of boats – gaily painted,... and still enhance many a bathroom shelf!"[2]

In the 1970s his work was exhibited more widely and he began to be able to make larger works, many of them with moving parts. Probably the finest of these, certainly the most characteristic, is *Bathers*, which drew its inspiration directly from the ocean liners that sailed down Southampton Water in the heyday of sea travel.

We cannot leave this review of art inspired by the landscape of Hampshire without a mention of probably Britain's best loved modern cartoonist, Norman Thelwell. Thelwell, who lives in the valley of the River Test, has produced numerous books of cartoons portraying the absurdities of rural life. Whilst none of them show actual localities, inspiration has clearly been drawn from the countryside of Hampshire, in particular the trout rivers of the Test and the Itchen, and the New Forest. His love of the Hampshire countryside can be seen in his watercolours of Winchester, Mottisfont and the River Test.

The majority of the artists who have been referred to in this chapter are represented in the collection of Southampton Art Gallery, which probably has the best collection of nineteenth- and twentieth-century art in any gallery in the south of England, outside London, as well as having many important works from other centuries.

The collection does contain works of Hampshire scenes but the

Classical statue at Mottisfont Abbey

importance of the collection is not parochial, and it is one of Hampshire's cultural glories.

Sculpture accounts for the majority of the art in Hampshire which does not specifically draw its inspiration from the county but which nevertheless contributes to its cultural interest. As we have seen, the early history of sculpture was closely associated with architecture and the decoration of buildings. It was only when, in the eighteenth century, public monuments and garden statuary became popular that sculpture became divorced from architecture to any significant degree.

The eighteenth-century connoisseur was particularly interested in the classical and antique and this led to the siting of figures from classical mythology in gardens. Typical examples can be seen in the gardens of Mottisfont Abbey. Finest of the eighteenth-century public monuments in Hampshire is the statue of William III in the Square at

Statue of William III, The Square, Petersfield

Petersfield. Fabricated in lead, and originally gilded, it was made by John Cheer in 1757 and first stood in the grounds of Petersfield House.

The fashion for public monuments reached its height in the nineteenth century. A fine and indeed dramatic example of this can be seen in the Wellington Monument by Matthew Cotes Wyatt. Originally made in the 1840s for the top of the Constitution Arch in London, it can now be found on a bluff near All Saints Church, Aldershot. The Great Hall in Winchester is home to Alfred Gilbert's Jubilee statue of the enthroned Queen Victoria. Unveiled in 1887 this originally stood outside the Great Hall. Lavishly decorated and embellished with allegorical figures which represent the arts and sciences, this work is an early example of the extravagant figure ornamentation which reached its height in the Edwardian period.

Other important public monuments in Hampshire include the statue of the hymn writer, Isaac Watts, carved in stone by Richard Cockle Lucas in 1861, situated in Watts Park, Southampton. This park also houses the tall rectangular Cenotaph made of Portland stone by Edwin Lutyens and, across the road, the memorial to the Titanic Engineers, which is a good example of early twentieth-century work. In Portsmouth, the Royal Naval War Memorial on the sea front at Southsea is a landmark from a considerable distance. Designed by Sir Robert Lorrimer, and erected in the early 1920s, "it is a splendidly balanced composition."[3]

In the second half of the twentieth century an increasing number of sculptures and other works of art have been sited in public places in Hampshire. For example, several works can be seen on the campus of Southampton University. Here buildings and sculpture have been sited together in a park-like environment. Notable among them are the *Two Figures* in bronze by Barbara Hepworth and *Sentinel* by John Edwards. Other examples from elsewhere in the county include the *Still Life* by Peter Randall Page, commissioned for the shopping centre at Chineham, Basingstoke, and the bronze *Horse and Rider* by Dame Elisabeth Frink, which was cast in 1975, and which has become a local landmark in Winchester High Street. All these works are good examples of how sculpture can help to create a sense of place.

From the time that William Gilpin saw the 'picturesque' in the landscape of the New Forest, artists have sought to portray the variety of Hampshire, from the hop-pickers of Bentley to warships anchored at Spithead, from Netley Abbey to the Itchen Floating Bridge, and from disappearing farming methods to ocean liners on Southampton Water. Before that, artists may not have responded to their surroundings in the same way but the wealth created in Hampshire provided the means for artists to work in centres of power, such as Winchester, and create, for example the great works of Anglo-Saxon and Norman art.

Having explored the art of Hampshire we turn finally in this chapter to music. Here there is considerably less to distinguish the county, at least as far as composers are concerned, than in the fields of art and literature. Few composers of note have been born in the county and Hampshire does not appear to have had the same effect on composers as it has on writers and painters. Even in the great period of English romantic music which extended from the end of the nineteenth century into the first half of the twentieth century, few composers drew inspiration from the county.

We do, however, have to go back again to Saxon Winchester for Hampshire's earliest musical connections. Before modern musical notation and, of course, recording, music was one of the most ephemeral of the arts; so the importance of Saxon music is not so widely known as, for example, their sculpture or manuscripts. However, the Winchester Tropes, which were ornamental additions to plainsong music, were influential and of national significance at the time, although they did not survive after the Norman Conquest.

The pealing of church bells was confirmed in a provision made at a synod held in Winchester in 970 – asserting Winchester's importance in the cultural life of the nation at that period. However the sound made by church bells at that time would have been very different from what we hear today. It was only after the Reformation that the method of hanging bells changed, allowing them to be rung in a controlled pattern, and the sound we know today began to evolve. In Saxon times the bells were swung and produced a random sequence of notes – more akin to French and Spanish churches today.

Hampshire has had, over the centuries, a particular link with religious music. Sternhold, a Court poet in the sixteenth century who translated the psalms and set them to the metre that is still used in the Anglican Church, lived at Hursley. Three well-known hymn writers lived in the county. Isaac Watts was born in Southampton in 1674 and wrote his early hymns for use in the chapel in Above Bar where his father served as a deacon. Watts is regarded as the father of English hymn writing. The best known of his hymns is *O God Our Help in Ages Past.* Among others he wrote in the early eighteenth century was *There is a Land of Pure Delight,* which contains the lines:

"Sweet fields beyond the swelling flood
Stand dressed in living green..."

There is a story that he wrote the lines looking out from above Southampton to the Isle of Wight. Another version of the story has him looking across Southampton Water to Eling and the New Forest! Also writing in the eighteenth century,

Barley field near Petersfield

Anne Steele was a member of the Baptist Church at Broughton. She wrote more than a hundred hymns, best known of which are *Father, whate'er of earthly bliss* and *Father of mercies, in Thy Word / What endless glory shines.* In the nineteenth century John Keble, leader of the Oxford Movement, published his cycle of hymns, *The Christian Year*, when he was vicar of Hursley.

We will be looking at some of Hampshire's folk songs in the next chapter but it was in a popular vein that Charles Dibdin, born in Southampton, composed his numerous sea shanties, inspired by the Hampshire coast.

Best known among these are songs like *Tom Bowling* and *Poor Jack* which were said to have done more for recruiting into the Royal Navy than the press gangs! *Tom Bowling*, which has much in common with the pop songs of the late twentieth century which romanticise death, starts with the words:

"Here, a sheer hulk, lies poor Tom Bowling,
The darling of our crew;
No more he'll hear the tempest howling,
For Death has broached him to."

and ends:

"Thus Death, who Kings and tars dispatches,
In vain Tom's life has doffed,
For, though his body's under hatches,
His soul is gone aloft."

Classical composers were drawing inspiration from the landscape as early as the beginning of the nineteenth century. Mendelssohn, for example, wrote his concert overture, Hebrides, in 1830. However it was not until the end of the nineteenth century that English romantic music really came into its own. This movement continued well into the twentieth century with composers such as Elgar, Butterworth, Delius, Vaughan Williams and Finzi. Of these composers it is only Gerald Finzi who had connections with Hampshire.

Gerald Finzi was born in London in 1901. After a musical education in London he moved to Painswick in Gloucestershire, drawn by the landscape of Elgar, Gurney and Vaughan Williams. After a further spell in London, he moved in 1935 to Aldborne in Wiltshire, and in 1937 to Hampshire where he settled in Ashmansworth. Much of his music was composed there, including his clarinet and cello concertos and his major choral work, *In Terra Pax.*

Finzi died in Oxford in 1956. It is difficult to discover a sense of place that is recognizably Hampshire in Finzi's music, although a feeling for the English landscape underscores every note, but as his best music was written in this corner of England it is, I think, acceptable to see in it the hills and valleys of the North Hampshire Downs in which he found a home.

Gustav Holst included folk songs from Hampshire in his *Second Suite for Military Band in F*, while Walton's overture *Portsmouth Point* was inspired by Portsmouth's naval heritage.

Above Bar Street, Southampton

HAMPSHIRE LIFE

At the beginning of this book I suggested that if a visitor was parachuted into Hampshire without map and compass they could find out where they were by the landscape and architecture of the area. It would, of course, have been easier for the visitor to ask the first person he or she met! As well as being told where they had landed, the visitor might pick up clues as to the location from the accent and dialect of the speaker. In this chapter we look at the people of Hampshire, their traditions, customs and food, and their words and songs.

Starting with the people themselves, it would be very difficult today, if not impossible, to distinguish Hampshire people from other English people by their looks. Yet as recently as the beginning of the twentieth century W. H. Hudson commented that,

"on going directly from any other district in Southern England to the central part of Hampshire one is sensible to a difference in the people." [1]

The Hampshire accent does, on the other hand, still differ from that of neighbouring counties, and even within the county. People such as John Arlott brought the Hampshire accent to millions through his cricket commentaries and other broadcasts. The soft Hampshire accent is less easily placed, or mimicked for that matter, than that of other regional accents, and this is partly due to the position of Hampshire in central southern England. The accent is a transitional one, having much in common with the West Country accents of Dorset and Wiltshire, whilst at the same time being influenced by the accents of counties to the north and east of Hampshire. The most obvious link with other West Country accents is the pronunciation of the 's' as 'z' in words like 'sing'. However, individual sounds and habits link the Hampshire accent with other counties. For instance the whole county shares with Berkshire, but not the West Country, the habit of adding an 's' to verbs, as in 'they goes'.

Hampshire people have been known for several centuries as Hampshire Hogs, an association that arose out of the county's fame for the breeding of pigs. For example, in 1662, Fuller wrote the following:

"Hampshire hogs are allowed by all for the best bacon... Here the swine feed in the forest on plenty of acorns... which, going out lean, return home fat, without care or cost to their owners. Nothing but fulness stinteth their feeding on the mast falling from the trees, where also they lodge at liberty (not pent up, as in other places, to stacks of peas) which some assign the reason for the fineness of their flesh."

Later in the seventeenth century Morden repeated the eulogy, calling Hampshire hogs "the sweetest in the Kingdom".

Hampshire bacon did not just come from the New Forest where the pigs could roam free in the woods. Elsewhere in the county it was thought that the appetizing flavour of the bacon and hams depended on the

Pigs in the New Forest

pigs having access to the orchards where they fed on windfall apples. However, in view of the fact that not all of the pigs could have had access to either the Forest or orchards, the flavour most likely stemmed from the Hampshire breed itself, now extinct, and the method of curing used in the county.

Not surprisingly, William Cobbett commented on the subject in *Rural Rides*, noting that Hampshire pigs were "the very best meat that England contains". Cobbett himself was portrayed in cartoons in an uncomplimentary way as a Hampshire Hog with a devil's forked tail, and a Tory adversary said of him,

> "if he had not been pointed out to me by one who knew him, I should probably have passed him over as one of the innocent bacon-eaters of the New Forest."

Evidently in the slump of 1821 Hampshire's reputation was kept up by the corn-fed hogs of Uphusband, near Andover.

Elsewhere Cobbett noted that

Watercress beds, near Alresford

STRAWBERRY FIELDS, NEAR HEDGE END

Hampshire was "not much of a cheese county", nor are there any indigenous breeds of cattle. In the nineteenth century, for example, Vancouver refers to Guernsey cattle at Lymington and Milford and, in the late eighteenth century, when Jane Austen was a child at Steventon, her father kept five Alderney cows.

Hampshire's other renowned food products are strawberries, trout and watercress. Mention was made in the second chapter of the pure waters of the chalk streams and rivers of Hampshire that have produced perfect conditions for the growing of watercress and the rearing of trout.

The earliest reference to strawberry growing in the county is 1287, when the reeve at Compton paid a rent of a measure of strawberries to be delivered each year to the infirmary of the Priory of St Swithun, Winchester. However it was not until the mid nineteenth century that they were grown on an extensive scale. Then the commons between Southampton and

Advertising hoarding for Strong's Ales (photo: Whitbread plc)

Fareham were enclosed and it was found that the soil was particularly suitable for the growing of strawberries. Here, in warm, sheltered conditions, strawberries could be supplied early in the season to the London market made easily and speedily accessible by the coming of the railways. Villages such as Hedge End, Swanwick, Sarisbury Green and Lock's Heath expanded at this time as a result of the strawberry growing industry.

Particular parts of the county have specialized in certain food products, either because of soil and climate, as in the case of strawberries around Fareham, or because of their proximity to markets. A considerable area in the south-east of the county, for instance, was used to provide provisions for the Royal Navy in Portsmouth and Gosport. The area between Alton, in East Hampshire, and Farnham, just over the border in Surrey, was one of England's hop-gardens. The distinctive fields of hops growing on wires stretched between tall hop poles have now largely disappeared. Beer is still brewed in the county, although the majority of the eighty breweries that existed in 1900 have disappeared. Beer could be said to be the taste of the region, the quality and hardness of the water being important in making bitter. Thus Romsey on the Test, Ringwood on the Avon, and Alton on the Wey all became centres for the brewing industry. Alton was also well positioned to supply London. Today the main Hampshire breweries are Whitbreads and Gales but the brewery most associated with Hampshire was Strongs, with its advertising hoarding telling us that we were in the Strong Country. For generations of Londoners driving westwards for their holidays this sign became inextricably associated with the good times they were about to experience.

I cannot leave food grown in Hampshire without a brief mention of sea kale, which is one of the few vegetables which has been developed from the native British Flora. Geoffrey Grigson says of it,

"before cultivation began, Sea Kale had probably been an English wild food for hundreds of years... In Hampshire, on the long sands by Calshot Castle, the country people watched for the young shoots to appear, heaped sand around them to blanch out their bitterness, and collected bundles to dispose of in Southampton."[2]

It was a Hampshire man, the botanist William Curtis, who, in the eighteenth century, popularized Sea Kale by writing a pamphlet of *Directions for the Culture of the Crambe Maritima or Sea Kale, for the use of the Table.*

A book by local people published in the 1930s alleged that "Hampshire seems to have very few specialities in the way of cakes, etc"[3]. However, Kate Easlea, in her book on Hampshire cooking, wrote that,

"the standard and variety of cooking in Hampshire can compare very favourably with those in other counties of Great

Britain, but for too many years have remained in the background."[4]

Inevitably most of the notable recipes take Hampshire specialities as their base, so we get recipes for watercress soup, and watercress sauces to be used with trout. Similarly it is not surprising to find recipes for Hampshire Gammon and Apricot Pie, Hampshire Bacon and Onion Roll, or Pork and Apple Pie. Nor is it unusual to find recipes using venison.

Pork is the main ingredient in Hampshire Haslet. In this, stale bread is soaked in milk, mixed with pork, onion and seasoning, baked in a loaf tin and served cold with salad. Pig's Head Cheese uses the meat removed from a boiled pig's head, minced and mixed with seasoning and herbs, which is pressed in a colander and again served cold. A pig's head was also an essential ingredient of Hampshire Cottage Broth. Both these recipes originate in the custom of keeping a house pig for domestic use.

Turning to sweet things, the recipe for Hampshire lardy cakes differs from lardy cakes made elsewhere in the country in that it should not contain fruit – only bread dough, lard, sugar and salt. In Hampshire, Gingerbread Men are called Gingerbread Husbands, and include currants and cherries. Traditional recipes for puddings included the delightful sounding Friars Omelette, made with baked apples, butter, sugar and egg yolks, and Brown Bread and Honey Ice Cream which used to be served in Winchester College Tuck Shop. Reputedly the recipe was a closely guarded secret until recently.

The individuality of an area is most clearly defined by its customs and one of the most traditional in England is that of the mummers. Hampshire had many more groups than the average county – well over seventy villages are known to have had mummers and each had its own version of the play. The earliest known play in Hampshire, from Romsey, dates from around 1800 but the origins of mummers plays are much older. Mumming more or less died out throughout the country at the time of the First World War but does survive, or has at least been revived, in a few places in Hampshire.

A tradition that is at least as old as the early 1700s is that of hanging Maidens' Garlands in the church at Abbotts Ann, near Andover. Over forty garlands are hung along the walls of the nave just under the ceiling. These crown-like garlands, made of hazel and paper flowers, were carried at the funerals of people who were born, baptised, confirmed in the parish and died virgins. Paper gloves were hung from the crowns representing a challenge to anyone who threw doubt on the character of the dead person. In most churches only young girls were so honoured but in Abbotts Ann young men also received a garland. The latest is dated 1973 and Abbotts Ann is apparently the only place where this custom survives.

Maidens' Garlands in Abbotts Ann Church

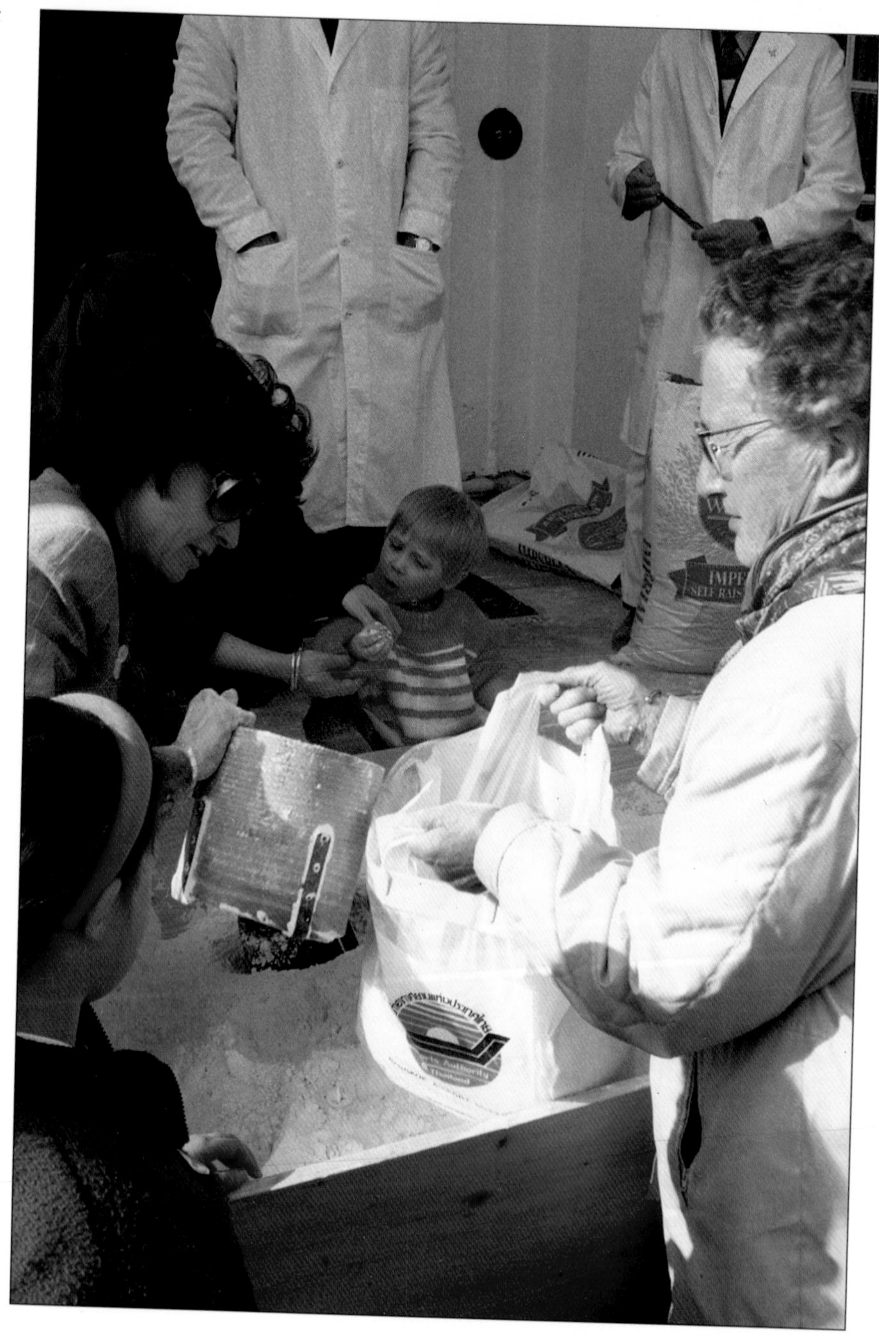

Giving out the Dole, Tichborne (Photo: the author)

An older tradition is that of the Tichborne Dole. The story is that in the fifteenth century Lady Mabel de Tichborne, when on her death bed, requested that the value of a small portion of the estates should be given annually to the poor of the district. Her husband, who was not of a very charitable nature, said that he would give the value of as much land as she could get round while holding a flaming torch. The lady, who was almost a cripple, succeeded in circumventing twenty three acres of land, crawling most of the way on all fours. Before she died she insisted that if ever the tradition of giving dole to the value of that piece of land, still known as 'The Crawls', was stopped seven sons would be borne to the family followed by a generation of seven daughters, when the name would die out and the house would fall down.

The custom of distributing the dole, in the form of bread, continued, apparently without a break, until 1794, when it was stopped because it was attracting tramps and vagabonds from all over England. At the time there were seven sons, four of whom subsequently died, either unmarried, or without sons. In 1802 the old house partly fell and was partly pulled down. Henry, the eldest son, had seven daughters but no sons and, not surprisingly Edward, another son, reinstated the ceremony in 1836.

Today the dole is distributed each Lady Day in the form of flour, at one time made from wheat grown on the estate, to the inhabitants of the parishes of Tichborne, Cheriton and Lane End, adults receiving one gallon of flour and children half a gallon, with a maximum of four gallons to a family.

In Portsmouth, on Trafalgar Day, Portsmouth citizens led by the Lord Mayor still process to lay a wreath on the statue to Lord Nelson. In the Dockyard the Victory is decorated with garlands and a wreath is laid on the deck at the spot where he was struck down. Nelson's famous signal is flown by all the ships in the dockyard. The continuance of these traditions nearly two hundred years after the event they commemorate demonstrates the place Nelson holds in the nation's consciousness, a place that, at least in his lifetime, led the people to believe that he could deliver the country from any external threat in the same way that King Arthur had done in legend.

Ancient courts survive both in the New Forest and at Stockbridge. Those at Stockbridge, the Courts Leet and Baron, are held each year in March and are unique. Jurors are appointed by the commoners, known as Burgesses, of the Manor of Stockbridge to settle the 'stint' – that is, arrange the dates when grazing is permitted – and bring forward criticisms of the management of the grazing on Stockbridge Down and Stockbridge Marsh. Officials are also appointed to, among other things, collect the fees for grazing. The history of the Manor of Stockbridge goes back almost to the Norman Conquest but the Courts still serve a useful function in settling the affairs of the Manor.

Two very different customs survive in Southampton. The first takes place each May Day morning when the choir of King Edward VI School sing May carols from the Bargate at, or at least soon after, dawn. After singing a number of carols, flowers are thrown to those listening below. The origins of this ceremony are unknown but according to tradition the Bargate has long been used in this way. The custom lapsed in the nineteenth century but it was revived early in the twentieth century by the Rector of St Mary's. It again lapsed during the Second World War and was revived in 1957. In recent years King John's Morris have danced on the same morning at the foot of the Bargate before the choristers arrive.

In the centre of Southampton, near the Dock Gates, is reputedly the

Knights of the Green,
Old Bowling Club, Southampton

world's oldest bowling green. There has been a lawn there since 1187 but it was not used regularly for bowls until the first Master of the Green was appointed in 1299. Each year members of the club compete over a number of days for the privilege of becoming a Knight of the Green, supervised by those who have won in previous years, the Knights, dressed in formal morning attire.

Cricket, "the game the wealden rustics handed down"[5], has long been associated with Hampshire, and the name of Hambledon has a particularly important place in cricket history. However, as John Arlott pointed out, "Hambledon has often carelessly and wrongly been called 'the cradle of cricket'"[6]. Cricket had its origins in a hundred different places, although its early history appears to be particularly associated with the downlands of Kent, Sussex and Hampshire. It is on record that the boys of Winchester College were playing a form of the game on St Catherine's Hill in the

CRICKET ON BROADHALFPENNY DOWN

Fishing hut on the River Test, near Longstock

1640s. Hambledon became the first major centre for serious cricket and substantial contemporary accounts exist of the game being played there. It is this that has given it a special place in the history of the game.

In an earlier chapter we noted that the landscape of Hampshire, in particular the continued existence of shelter belts, owed much to its use for sport. It is doubtful, though, whether the landscape in Hampshire was altered for hunting to the extent Linda Colley describes in her book *Britons*:

"The very scenery of Great Britain was now re-organised and re-envisioned in keeping with the leisure priorities of men of land and substance. Hedges were torn down, ditches filled, gates and bridges built, tenants privacy invaded, all in pursuit of the unfortunate, uneatable fox."

Hampshire does however have a place in the history of hunting, again on account of its connections with wealth and power. Not only did it boast one of the earliest regular packs of foxhounds, a pack being kept at

Breamore as early as 1690, but it was royal patronage of foxhunting in Hampshire that led it to become universally popular among the gentry. The shift in fashion was marked by the Prince of Wales, afterwards George IV, changing his staghounds to foxhounds in 1793. The Prince of Wales regularly hunted in Hampshire, leasing Kempshott Park in 1788 and Northington Grange in 1795. All the main hunts in Hampshire were started in the late eighteenth century, the earliest being the Hampshire Hunt whose forerunner came into being in 1745.

Children, as revealed by the Opies in their studies[7], can be an important channel for tradition. Games are still played in school playgrounds, jokes told and songs sung, but with television providing the main source of material there are, no doubt, fewer regional variations. It is doubtful, for example, whether practices, such as the following still exist:

"In villages around Alton, and as far away as East Meon, near Petersfield, at Crowborough in Sussex, and doubtless in other places, children pick up a black-budded twig of ash and put it in their pockets on this day. A child who does not remember to bring a piece of ash to school on Ash Wednesday can expect to have his feet trodden on by every child who possesses a twig, unless, that is, he or she is lucky enough to escape until midday."[8]

Nor is 'spotted dick' likely still to be served in a roly-poly shape, if served at all, in Portsmouth schools, and therefore the children's name for it, 'Bugs in the Bolster', will have fallen into disuse.

One regional difference described by the Opies does appear still to be found in the playgrounds of Hampshire schools, and this is the use of 'truce' words. In Hampshire 'scribs' is the predominant term, with others such as 'squibs' and 'scrims' being found as variants.

Vocabulary in various parts of the country used to be full of regional variations. For example, Geoffrey Grigson collected numerous different local names for flowers and trees in his *Englishman's Flora*, from which a picture emerges of how local language used to be. Many plants in the *Flora* have, in their lists of names, ones that are unique to Hampshire.

A number of these names are associated with Hampshire's seafaring past, such as Greater Stitchwort, often known as Shirt Buttons, called here Sailor's Buttons. Creeping Jenny was Roving Sailor, Ivy Leafed Toadflax was Travelling Sailor, and Mugwort, the leaves of which were often smoked, was Sailor's Tobacco. Trees particularly associated with Hampshire also had local names; yew, for example, was Hampshire Weed, showing how common it once was. The hawthorn was known as Hog-Berry or Hog-Haw, the name of which, although it also became known as Pig-Haw, did not derive from Hampshire's association with hogs but rather the Old English 'Haeg', meaning fruit. Similarly the

The Camber, Old Portsmouth

blackthorn was known as Pig in the Hedge or Hedgepicks!

Every county in Britain has its folk songs and Hampshire is no exception. As is usual with folk songs many of them have local connections. Hampshire's seafaring links with the most famous naval battle in history is celebrated in *The Battle of Trafalgar*, and its links with the military in songs such as *I'm a Bold and Roving Soldier*. Events which took place in Hampshire are recorded in ballads such as *The Execution of Frederick Baker*. Baker's name is forgotten today but the girl he murdered in a hop field near Alton, Fanny Adams, is not. The execution of Alice Lisle is remembered in *The Monmouth Rebel*, and those hung or transported for taking part in the 'Swing' farm riots of 1830 in *The Owslebury Lads*.

There is no such thing as a Hampshire anthem, although *Down Hampshire Way*, written in the 1920s, was no doubt intended to serve as such, opening with the words:

"I'm Hampshire bred and Hampshire born,
And proud of it am I,
No softer, purer air I know
Beneath God's boundless sky ...."

and ending with the chorus:

"Go east, go west, old Hampshire's best
And all therein is fine
If Hampshire highways and byways are my ways,
They always will be mine!"

This song was no doubt intended to be taken seriously but not all the songs written about places in Hampshire were, as can be seen from this extract from a song about Gosport:

"I sing not of Naples, of Venice, or Rome,
Of the pillars of Trojan or Peter's fine dome;
Neither praise I old Brentford, that place of renown,
But will sing of a seaport, and Gosport's the town.
"And the inns are so noble, so neat and so clean,
If you talk of a mop they scarce know what you mean;
All infection however, they keep from their doors,
With tobacco juice sprinkled to sweeten the floors."

And so on for another six verses!

At this stage, if this book were being written elsewhere in Europe, or even in Wales or Scotland, we would be turning to traditional dress. In England today there is no such thing. However, as recently as the nineteenth century, agricultural labourers often wore a functional smock-frock. A long, loose, linen over-gown, the smock was popular among farm labourers and carters. Although motifs on the smocks reflected the trade of the wearer – wheels for carters and waggoners, trees and leaves for woodmen, flowers for gardeners, and crooks for shepherds – in looking at the smock-frock we do find regional differences.

Working smocks in the Midlands were characteristically blue, and those in Hertfordshire olive green, those in central southern England were natural

Hurdle making near Little Somborne

flax coloured or white – a colour reserved further north for Sunday best, weddings and funerals. The main feature that distinguishes Hampshire smocks from other English examples seems to be a double- or even triple-layered collar split behind, at the nape of the neck as well as the collarbone.

Regional differences exist in the production of agricultural and horticultural tools, with individual designs for a Hampshire billhook, a Hampshire hurdling hook, and a Hampshire hoe. There also used to be differences in farm vehicles. Vancouver's *Agricultural History of Hampshire,* published in 1810, illustrates a Hampshire wagon. This book also has a picture of a Hampshire gate, whose solid wooden construction bears no relation at all to the so-called 'Hampshire gate' of today's farmers made from barbed wire strung across a field entrance!

In a few places in Hampshire, woodmen can still be found making hurdles and other products from

Hurdle making near Little Somborne

coppiced woods. It is interesting to note that the hurdle most usually produced in Hampshire has nine 'sails' or uprights in contrast to the Dorset hurdle of eight and the Wiltshire hurdle which has ten. So, if all else failed, our visitor parachuted into the wilds of Hampshire could look at the nearest hurdle that might be filling a gap in the hedge or surrounding a sheep pen and check how many uprights it had!

Fields near Winchester

CHAPTER 7

A FUTURE FOR HAMPSHIRE

ALL THROUGH THIS BOOK we have been looking at those elements of the Hampshire landscape and architecture, its people, art, literature, music, customs and other things that make it distinctive. The same thing could have been done for any county or region in Britain. We all recognize regional differences when looking at Scotland or Wales, Cornwall and the West of England, the Lake District, Northumbria or the Yorkshire Dales. But when it comes to the South we tend to see it as a fairly uniform area with little to distinguish one county from another. We all see local differences in the landscape but it is not usually accepted that each county has a distinctive character. I hope, however, that I have shown in the course of this book that this is untrue. In an area like Hampshire, where there are significant pressures for development and where the individuality of the area may not be recognised, vernacular cultures are under the greatest pressure.

Hampshire contains some of the best landscape in the south of England, which, whilst not as spectacular as that to be found in other parts of the country, is richly satisfying. From the woodlands and heaths of the New Forest, through river valleys to the downs and the coast, it is the variety of landscape that makes Hampshire unique. Hampshire's clear chalk streams, sought out by anglers, are the purest in the country. Its downland, whilst not seeming so wild today as it did when William Cobbett rode across it on his *Rural Rides*, is still some of the remotest landscape in the south. The harbours have seen all of the great ships of the navy, from the *Mary Rose* to the *Ark Royal*, the Cunarders and other great liners, and one of the biggest invasion fleets in history assembled in 1944 in the sheltered waters of the Solent, which are now a mecca for yachtsmen.

These landscapes are under constant threat. The population of Hampshire has almost trebled since 1900 and increased by fifty per cent since the 1950s. All the major towns and cities have grown considerably, and the spread of the motor car has enabled many villages to become homes to people commuting to nearby towns or to London. The increase in the number of cars has brought the need to widen roads and provide by-passes. Motorways have had the most dramatic effect on the landscape but every road widening scheme and by-pass has led to some alteration. Motorways are built to national standards of gradients and widths and travelling along either the M3 or M27 little of the 'real' countryside of Hampshire can be seen. The lack of respect that motorway design has for the countryside can most dramatically be seen in the cutting through Twyford Down made to complete the M3 around Winchester.

Modern farming methods, especially the use of larger and larger

continued on page 131

East meon

CONSTRUCTION OF M3 EXTENSION, TWYFORD DOWN, NEAR WINCHESTER

Field near East Tisted

continued from page 127

machinery, has led to an increase in the size of fields and the consequent loss of hedges between fields. Where farmers have gone over entirely to growing grain and other cereal crops, even boundary hedges have been lost. This process is nothing new. As long ago as the early nineteenth century Cobbett bemoaned the fact that farms in North Hampshire were being merged. He would, however, have been surprised by the size fields have reached today. Fields in the cereal areas of Hampshire can be as big as a hundred and fifty acres.

The character of the landscape is not entirely without protection. The designation of parts of the downs and river valleys as Environmentally Sensitive Areas is compensating farmers for the loss of income they experience in agreeing to farm these important landscapes by traditional methods. Hedge planting schemes are restoring the boundaries of fields and new pockets of woodland are being planted on farm land being removed from cultivation. So long as trees native to the county are being used this will help maintain its character.

When we turn to architecture, it is not the major monuments, such as Winchester Cathedral, Romsey Abbey or Portchester Castle, we have to worry about or, on the whole, those buildings which have received official recognition through listing. The character of an area is given, not so much by these buildings, as by vernacular architecture. Here there are two threats. First, through the changes that can be made to existing buildings by alterations, extensions, or demolition; second through new building which has little regional individuality.

In the chapter on architecture we noted that changes to vernacular architecture began when the improvements to transport brought first the canals and then the railways to Hampshire. This enabled cheaper, more durable, or more easily worked building materials to be used in domestic buildings. Prior to this they were mainly made of materials that were obtained locally. Styles of construction varied around the country and, even where bricks were used, because they had been made locally, they differed in colour, shape and size.

Existing vernacular architecture is threatened in several ways. Industrial buildings have often ceased to serve the purpose for which they were built; when this happens they are often demolished or, if they are kept, are altered to such an extent that their original use is obscured. Sometimes, though, they can be restored and given new commercial life similar to the original purpose, as has happened at Whitchurch Silk Mill, or they have been restored as working museums, as at Bursledon Windmill and Eling Tide Mill.

Traditional farm buildings are similarly threatened in that they are rarely suitable for modern farming methods or large enough to house

continued on page 134

A panel depicting The Wallops from the Test Valley Tapestry (photo: Test Valley Borough Council)

A panel depicting Amport from the Test Valley Tapestry
(photo: Test Valley Borough Council)

continued from page 131

present day farm machinery. In this case they are likely to be abandoned to decay. Some have been given new life as light industrial units or have been converted to housing but in either case the result rarely bears any relationship to the original purpose of the building. When surrounded by newly laid out gardens, or when, in the case of the industrial units, the need for parking has been taken into account and surrounding roads have been adapted for the additional traffic generated, the integrity of the countryside is further compromised.

The character of houses and cottages is threatened by extensions which, whether or not they are sympathetic, change the scale of the building and belie its humble origins. How many 'Keeper's Cottages' are there in Hampshire, for instance, which are now more akin to mansions than the homes of river bailiffs? Not only can these changes in scale dramatically alter the street and village scene but they can alter the make-up of private housing in a community to the extent that the one and two-bedroomed cottages that provide many people with their first homes are no longer available and specific action has to be taken in order to redress the balance.

Not only do building materials give domestic architecture its character and individuality but so do the style of windows, doors and chimneys. Here the replacement of original windows with double glazing, often with p.v.c. frames, the use of inappropriate standardized doors, the removal of chimneys when no longer needed, the addition of standard porches and conservatories, all serve to reduce the individuality of even the most characteristic house.

Proportionally, though, it is the building of new houses that is having the most effect on the individuality of vernacular architecture. Over six thousand houses are being built each year in Hampshire. Most of these are being built to designs which are little different from those being used elsewhere in the country, and local materials are rarely used. Where the designer does try to give the houses some individuality it is usually by adding mock-Tudor or Victorian fronts or by the use of mock leaded windows or stained glass. None of these features have any historical accuracy and overlook the simplest methods of giving individuality to a new building – the use of vernacular styles and materials.

Culture is not just about landscape and architecture. Culture is about people. Culture is everything that defines our existence and gives meaning to our lives, and so it includes the language, games and songs of the people themselves. Here variety is being lost through the influence of press, television and films, which spread a universal mono-culture, through rapid communications and economic mobility – which means, for example, that people on average move house

NEW HOUSING AT HORTON HEATH, SOUTHAMPTON

Whitchurch Silk Mill

every seven years. All these factors combine to make it much more difficult for local traditions to be passed down from one generation to the next and serve to iron out differences in accents, dialect and language.

It would be interesting to see an up-dated version of the research that Iona and Peter Opie produced in the 1950s on *The Lore and Language of School Children* but I am certain from my own observations that many of the regional variations and variety in children's games have disappeared under the influences referred to earlier.

Few customs or traditions have survived into the second half of the twentieth century. Oldest of the surviving customs is that of the Tichborne Dole and others, such as the singing of the May hymn from the Bargate in Southampton, were revived successfully after the Second World War. Recently an interest in traditional customs has led to the performing of

WEAVING AT THE SILK MILL

Sikh women celebrating Baisakhi Festival, Southampton

mummers plays in several villages, sometimes using local texts. Other customs, such as 'Decking the Bower' at Oakhanger, have also been revived. The popularity of revivals such as this show a yearning for a sense of belonging and for the spirit of place that such ceremonies represent.

Traditional Arts Projects, established in 1989, has played an important part in encouraging communities to develop and celebrate their own communities. These activities have taken the form of evenings of traditional song and dance, and workshops in mumming, long sword dancing and other similar activities in schools and villages. One interesting project that Traditional Arts Projects was involved in arose out of a community project in the Test Valley. During the 1980s, at the instigation of the then Mayor of Test Valley, all the villages and towns in the area combined to create a series of embroidered panels depicting life in the valley. To celebrate its completion Traditional Arts Projects commissioned an original piece of music from John Kirkpatrick which used, as its source material, Hampshire folk tunes.

Hampshire is further enriched by the cultures and traditions of the Black and Asian communities and other ethnic minority groups. The main minority communities are Pakistani, Indian, Bangladeshi, Afro-Caribbean and Chinese. There are also other smaller groups including Polish, Greek, Vietnamese and Cypriots, all contributing to a multi-racial society in Hampshire.

The majority of these groups began to settle in Southampton in the 1950s and 1960s, where there are now, as well as in Basingstoke, Aldershot and Portsmouth, second generation communities for whom Hampshire is home. For many, cultural and racial identity, together with links with their parents' birth place, holds great importance.

Many schools throughout Hampshire now take part in celebrating such festivals as the Chinese New Year, Diwali, Ramadan and Eid. Each year the Sikh community in Southampton celebrates its annual festival Baisakhi with a huge procession winding its way through the city centre, led by the Panj Pyare, the five beloved. These festivals and events are now as much a part of Hampshire culture as any others I have mentioned.

Artists, writers and sometimes musicians have drawn inspiration from Hampshire, whether or not they were born here. However much the artist loved the Hampshire landscape and was influenced by it, these are not examples of indigenous culture. Whilst the subject matter and inspiration may have been drawn locally, the style and form was metropolitan. The arts in Hampshire are lively and enjoy strong public support but as we approach the end of the twentieth century they remain metropolitan. Even where new work is

Weston Shore, Southampton Water

being created which will enhance the environment, many of the pieces being placed in public places are by artists from outside Hampshire. Although artists are being encouraged to work in the county, and studios are being provided, such as Artspace Studios in Portsmouth, the work owes more to national trends than local influences. This situation is likely to persist whilst London is seen to be the capital and main market for all the arts, and whilst regionalism is confused with parochialism to the detriment of work which has its roots in vernacular culture.

'Roots' is a word I have used only once before in this book, but it is a concept that should go naturally with culture. After all, 'culture' is the main part of both 'agriculture' and 'horticulture', and several of its meanings are associated with organic growth. People talk about 'putting down roots' when they move to a new area but for those roots to grow the ground has to be tended – or in this case the individuality of the area has to be protected, its history has to be understood and its culture cherished and celebrated.

I hope that this book will help the culture of Hampshire to be celebrated – a culture that is strong because of its variety. I do not want to see it preserved as some vast theme park. Its culture must go on developing, being enriched through the celebration of the different cultures contained within it. I want to see it open to influences from outside, from elsewhere in the country, from the rest of Europe and the world, open to these influences but not watered down by them. With the rich heritage that Hampshire has, and the liveliness of its culture today, it has nothing to fear from these influences.

We saw at the beginning of the book that Hampshire is a geographic and historic entity, I hope that it can also be seen that it has a cultural entity – one that makes it distinct from its neighbours. Hampshire has a unique variety of landscape, distinctive architecture and great masterpieces of art; many of the country's best known writers have written about it and painters have portrayed Hampshire scenes. Not only are these things worth celebrating and cherishing but also their continued existence means that our visitor who parachuted into the county without map and compass at the beginning of the book should have little trouble in working out where he or she has landed.

FOOTNOTES

Chapter 1

1 First pub. Willow Books, 1990

2 *The History of the English Shires* by James Campbell, pub. Hampshire County Council, 1993

3 First pub. J. M. Dent, 1932

4 *Notes towards the Definition of Culture,* pub. Faber and Faber, 1948

5 *The History of the English Shires* by James Campbell, pub. Hampshire County Council, 1993

Chapter 2

1 *A History of Hampshire* by Barbara Carpenter Turner, pub. Phillimore, 1973

2 *The Making of the English Landscape* by W. G. Hoskins, pub. Hodder and Stoughton, 1955

Chapter 3

1 *Hampshire and the Isle of Wight – Buildings of England* by Nikolaus Pevsner and David Lloyd, pub. Penguin, 1967

2 *Ibid.*

3 *Ibid.*

Chapter 4

1 from *Polyolbion*

2 *A Tour Through the Whole Island of Great Britain* by Daniel Defoe, 1724

3 *Ibid.*

4 *The South Country* by Edward Thomas, first pub. 1909

5 *Jane Austen's England* by Maggie Lane, pub. Hale, 1986

6 *The Peverel Papers* by Flora Thompson, pub. Century Hutchinson, 1986

Chapter 5

1 *Landscapes – an anthology from Southampton Art Gallery,* pub. Southampton Art Gallery, 1979

2 Gladys Smith, quoted in the catalogue for the Arts Council exhibition of Sam Smith's work, 1981

3 *The Buildings of England: Hampshire and the Isle of Wight* by Nikolaus Pevsner and David Lloyd, pub. Penguin, 1967

Chapter 6

1 *Hampshire Days* by W. H. Hudson, originally pub. 1903.

2 *The Englishman's Flora* by Geoffrey Grigson, pub. Phoenix House, 1958

3 *It Happened in Hampshire,* pub. Hampshire Federation of Women's Institutes, 1937

4 *Cooking in Hampshire Past and Present* by Kate Easlea, pub. Paul Cave, 1973

5 John Arlott

6 in the introduction to *From Hambledon to Lords,* edited by John Arlott, pub. Barry Shurlock, 1975

7 *Children's Games in Street and Playground* by Iona and Peter Opie, pub. Oxford, 1969

8 *Ibid.*

BIBLIOGRAPHY

Apart from the books referred to in the footnotes to the text, the following were used as background:

Man and the Landscape
Hampshire Countryside Heritage series No 8, pub. Hampshire County Council, 1984.

Four Centuries of Farming Systems in Hampshire, 1500-1900
by G. E. Russell, Papers and Proceedings of Hampshire Field Club, Vol XVII, 1949-52.

Hampshire, the Complete Guide
by Jo Draper, pub. Dovecote Press, 1990.

Pleasure Grounds – the Gardens and Landscapes of Hampshire
edited by Gill Hedley and Adrian Rance, pub. Milestones, 1987.

Houses in the Landscape – a Regional Study of Vernacular Building Styles in England and Wales
by John and Jane Penoyre, pub. Faber and Faber, 1978.

Parish Churches of England
by J. Charles Fox, pub. Batsford, 1935.

Sculpture in Hampshire
by Gordon Bradshaw and Garrick Palmer, pub. Hampshire County Council on behalf of the Hampshire Sculpture Trust, 1987.

Traditional Farm Buildings of Britain
by R. W. Brunskill, pub. Victor Gollancz, 1982.

Collected Poems
by Edward Thomas, first pub. 1909.

The Englishman's Flora
by Geoffrey Grigson, pub. Phoenix House Ltd, 1958.

The Life and Work of J. M. W. Turner
by Andrew Wilton, pub. Academy Editions, 1979.

Sir Alfred Munnings
by Stanley Booth, pub. Sotheby Parke Bernet Publications, 1978.

A History of Hunting in Hampshire
by Brigadier-General J. F. R. Hore, pub. Wykeham Press, 1950.

One Hundred Years of Progress
by Gillian A. Rushton, pub. Hampshire County Council, 1989.

Hampshire Country Recipes
by Ann Gomar, pub. Ravette Books, 1988.

English Custom and Usage
by Christina Hole, pub. Batsford, 1941.

National Trust Guide to Traditional Customs of Britain
by Brian Shuel, pub. Webb and Bower, 1985.

A History of Cricket in Hampshire
by Norman Gannaway, pub. Hampshire Books, 1990.

AUTHOR

PETER MASON has worked in Hampshire for the last thirteen years, living for most of this time in Broughton, in the Test Valley. He has been County Arts Officer for Hampshire County Council since 1985. His work in the arts has given him a wide interest in the culture and history of Hampshire and he has spoken on this at conferences in France and Italy.

Originally having trained for the theatre, he has worked in theatres in London, Salisbury and Exeter, for the Arvon Foundation in North Devon and, before moving to Hampshire, as Director of Salisbury Arts Centre.

He is a member of the Council of the Voluntary Arts Network, a Governor of the Winchester School of Art and a Fellow of the Royal Society of Arts.

PHOTOGRAPHER

JUDY HARRISON was born in Stoke-on-Trent in 1953. She studied photography at Manchester College of Art and Design and gained an M.A. in photography at the Royal College of Art.

After gaining an Arts Council Fellowship in 1977, when she became the first Fellow in Photography at Southampton University, she then founded and became Director of the successful Mount Pleasant Media Workshop from 1979 to 1992.

In 1986 she was invited to join FORMAT Women's Picture Agency, one of the leaders of social documentary photography, where she is now one of the core members.

Much of her social documentary photography has been published and exhibited nationally. Apart from working as a freelance photographer, she also lectures in photography and continues to run photography and media workshops.